Shimmering Japanese Sunlight

Musings on a Woman's Travels to Japan

Kay Thomas

Kay Thomas

ISBN – **13: 978-1536846591**

All photos are the property of the author.

Author information at Kathomaswriter.com

DEDICATION

To my tiger cat, Dickens, who waits home faithfully for my return.

To LRT, CB and PS.

To be a moral human being is to pay, be obliged to pay, certain kinds of attention. - Susan Sontag.

Experience the beauties of nature, and in doing so learn about yourself. – Unknown.

OTHER BOOKS

Travel

- *A Smidgen of Irish Luck*
A Woman's Musings on Her Travel to Ireland

Collected Newspaper Columns

- *AND ONE MORE THING*
I Brake for Squirrels and Other Thoughts I Have No Doubt About

- *AND ONE MORE THING, Volume II*
Don't Whatever Me, Ever

Essays

- *I'll Be Honest With You*

TABLE of CONTENTS

INTRODUCTION

ACKNOWLEDGMENTS

INTRODUCTION

If you are looking for a travel guide to Japan, keep searching. There are many excellent books written with suggestions on what to do, where to stay and overall useful pieces of pre-trip advice for any combination of travelers.

Fortunately, I downloaded a couple trusty ones to my computer for bringing along without dragging several extra precious pounds of cargo. Before setting out for the day, I reviewed highlights in preparation for excursions, and it helped in keeping one day from blending into the next—pretty soon I couldn't remember where I was two days ago, what the breakfast room at the previous hotel looked like and how many times I'd worn the same cargo pants—without my travel guide and the notes I hastily jotted on the computer.

Before I left home I set up a blog, *Tour Japan With Kay*, with the two-fold purpose of sharing pictures and short writings in real time with family and friends, and also, having a travel diary. I had a sneaking suspicion that there would be some heavy-duty writing coming out of this vacation when I returned to my desk, although I didn't expect I would stop everything so quickly—a moratorium went out on other writing assignments—and begin the chronicles in haste. There was just too much chatter in my head to ignore without going daffy, and I have learned that it is best to put everything aside not fighting the impulse. Since early spring, I desired a change of direction in my writing—a new challenging project.

This book is different on purpose. What I have tried to do is invite you into select experiences that I had on a visit to Japan, and my particular reactions—right or wrong—to them. I more or less wrote the strong memories that came to the surface in no chronological order, and I am sure that a fellow traveler on the same trip would have a whole different set of thoughts and wonder why I didn't discuss certain other highlights.

If I do my job, I will paint vivid pictures in your mind—from savoring raw tuna sushi near the bustling Tokyo wholesale fish market wishing I was headed to heaven right then and there, to a mountaintop morning with a Zen Buddhist priest—as you sit in your armchair, and reflect on which values are truly worthwhile personally at your own particular stage in life. You draw your conclusion about society in the 21st century, and how you might react to it in a deeper and more genuine way.

There is a thread running through the entire book that I didn't pick up on until I began revising my first draft. I speak passionately about quietness and how it heightens my senses to the moment. Often that is the point where my writing begins to flow on paper, and it defines me as a person. I feel quietness is a learned skill and I admire those who are further along the path perfecting and reaping the rewards of silence.

Shimmering Japanese Sunlight is not all seriousness, though. I do poke fun at my own fumbles—chopsticks can be a pain when you are tired, famished and left-handed—and my naive reactions—I should know better than to stare at fashionable women floating down the streets of Kyoto like I am surprised at the high-style of their clothing. If I can only remember to come to dinner at the resort in Hakone wearing my yukata—a cotton kimono style outfit—wrapped around me properly, I wouldn't get the chuckles from the rest of my group since I am prepared like a corpse with the left panel tucked in first. Thanks left-handedness. And I did it twice, too. Shame on me.

Three generations after World War II and the A-bombings in Hiroshima and Nagasaki, I wanted to put my thoughts to rest—I grew up hearing the stories and reading the history books—and pay tribute to efforts for peace on both sides. Reconciliation and healing are things of the past. Life moves on, and lessons are learned. That's why I decided to make the effort—long distance travel and lengthy air flights don't daunt me—to stand in those historic spots and breathe in the positive attitudes of goodwill for all.

I have been fortunate enough to travel many places in the world, and it always come down to this: it's all about the people. Always. We are citizens of the world from the Japanese children studying about World War II on a school field trip drawing conclusions for a modern era, to the sake makers worrying about the fermenting process and the housewives creating fabulous ikebana floral arrangements in their free moments. When our lives interact, it is beautiful. Our commonalities overshadow our differences. Our belief systems may be different; however, we foster love for one another and peace on earth.

Traveling for knowledge rather than information is the ideal approach for landing in a new destination. By carrying little baggage with you—I mean stereotypes and hearsay—you will delight in whatever you find. "The more I travel, the less I know. It's as simple as that." Anthony Bourdain, food critic and chef said those profound words during a TV episode on South Africa for *Anthony Bourdain: Parts Unknown.* I've heard that message said by other people; however, it came full circle for me while in Japan.

Going to Japan on your own, or as part of an organized tour—I went with Overseas Adventure Travel, affectionately known as OAT with 11 others—I trust you will find exploring the Land of the Rising Sun shining on you forever. This book gives you a glimpse of Japan from one woman's eyes.

The Art of Quiet

In exploring the myriad of sights in a colossal international city such as Tokyo, what impresses me the most is the quietness all around me. That sounds rather odd. You assume that commotion is part of a city's makeup and Tokyo would be no different. Tokyo is the exception, and how refreshing.

After all, people come to Japan to visit the magnificent shrines and temples, the Emperor's palace gardens and the National Museum within the city limits before expanding out to the rural countryside, Mount Fuji and the islands within this Pacific Ocean archipelago.

On top of that, I choose to come in the midst of Golden Week (a combination of several holidays including the Emperor's birthday) at the end of April—I am forewarned by a friendly salesperson as I book the trip—when Japanese folks are appreciating the season with time off, a rare treat for hard-working Japanese to spend time outside in the public parks. He suggests that I might as well get involved in the activities and see what the culture is all about. It makes perfect sense to me, and I assume that I will deal with the crowded conditions knowing full well the good outweighs the inconveniences.

Earlier in April the cherry blossoms were out in full force with another set of festivities around them, and what remains of them I would see in the higher elevations in Hakone. Now it is azaleas and purple and white of wisterias bleeding the landscape delicately like a Japanese watercolor of the Emperor's majestic garden. Thick clusters of wisteria drape over the wooden trellises and scent the air with heavy perfume. I am intoxicated with the serenity.

Quiet is little or no noise, and it evokes differing feelings.

Certain folks cannot tolerate quiet just like they can't stand to be alone with themselves for fear of getting in touch with their weaknesses, desires and perhaps, failures. If they don't have every minute of the day programmed, restlessness sets in. They become victims, rather than programmers of their own fate. It's easy to spot in someone—a quick look over Facebook posts for a week—and I want to shout, "Slow down and take it all in right in front of you."

Youth wants to be in two places at one time, and those married with children have to be in that boat rowing as fast as they can to keep things afloat. Those that age gracefully and let eldering take its course, look forward to select times for simple pleasures and nothing on the platter. It develops into a habit. The best of your ideas come at such times, new directions charted and an overall feeling of well-being exudes that shows in your physical appearance, too.

The quiet atmosphere is something that stands out significantly, though, and I want to explore that sensation of being mindful of the present without any distractions. In a city of 30 million by day when business is in operation and a population of 8 million, that is a lot of ants shifting from place to place in any twenty-four hour period. When I stand on a street and people move softly like robots to their destinations, I am certain I have found a most unusual lifestyle the opposite from what I have come to recognize as a city environment.

What's it like not to chatter incessantly with your fellow companions in a restaurant? As an alternative, you eat slowly and with heightened awareness.

How much more do you see and feel in a crowded art gallery when you wander alone through the rooms? You pick up on the nuances in the colors standing in different spots looking at the same piece of art.

Where does your mind go when it is free of noise pollution in a temple, church or shrine? It travels within and focuses on those precious in your life, or your recently deceased friend.

Rather, that peacefulness is all around me, and it leaves quite an impression at the start of a three-week trip. There is something about the location that catches me up, and frankly, I'm not expecting it at all. That awareness lasts my entire visit, and it does to this day weeks later while I write with a smile on my face. It is authentic for sure. Frankly, I like to be surprised and this trip puts me relatively at ease, which is a great way to be when you are far out of your comfort zone. I have read a lot of travel reviews and talks about Japan, and yet I have not seen anyone so captivated by the stillness as I came face–to-face with it. Instead, they will remark on efficiency, cleanliness and politeness, all those traits I agree with wholeheartedly.

In my anticipation of the trip I am concerned that the huge population so close to me squeezing in like an anchovy would overwhelm me on the streets, in subways and in restaurants until I got into a groove, or not.

Not that I hyperventilate in crowds, or anything of the sort, but it does make me slightly panicky. Once as a shrimp of a kid, I felt myself literally picked up and pushed through a crowd leaving the old Yankee Stadium in the Bronx, and I didn't like it one bit. Thank goodness I had my dad's hand firmly in place. That scary episode lingers with me, and puts me on guard in public.

Space is a premium that I take for granted. True, I spend a lot of time nowadays in an area where I am free of traffic, people and the usual sounds of town life. I have a heightened sensory awareness of my whereabouts for safety's sake, and when I leave for a town, city and travel, I know that I am required to up my level of attentiveness for a different reason. It's all good practice for keeping myself fit. I have established a fine balance, and I stay healthy, rested and mentally active that way.

The Japanese live within tight quarters, and respect the dignity of others, too. That's a win-win in my book. Since they appreciate other people, they don't trample on them physically or emotionally.

I shared college rooms and first apartments when my pocketbook was short of cash, and I tolerated others and their habits in order to get by. It's a way of living life that you either learn as a young child when you play with others, or you don't. Those bullies grow up and still torment in the workplace. The Japanese really don't know anything differently, and as my tour guide told me, America is rather frightening to her on the streets in Los Angeles and New York. It's all what you are accustomed to and how you can make adjustments when necessary.

Even the ownership of pets is regulated to one small dog in Tokyo, and at quite the price, too—a Pomeranian for seventy-six hundred American dollars. Then on the other hand, there are pet stores where you can befriend a pet for a time limit for a fee, and stroke and hug a cat or dog to your heart's content. I walk into a K-Mart like pet store with aisle upon aisle of accessories, color co-coordinated clothing and strollers, and it is over-the-top. A high regard for animals is more than a fad in Japan, and they are treated as celebrities most appreciated by their owners. A cuddly dog decked out in his Sunday best matching the color scheme of his owner, is out strolling in a pram along the wide walkway in the park. The interaction between pet and owner is priceless as the owner pulled out doggie snacks for him. Every pet should get that royal treatment.

When I land at Narita International Airport late in the evening, basic services—shops and restaurants—are closing and rolling down their security gates. Since mine is the last overseas flight, I am relatively free of the weary crowds pushing to get their passports stamped. Travelers are exhausted from the long haul flight, and I am no exception. I am thankful that I don't have any major decisions to make, or unnecessary rigmarole to face either like lost luggage. That makes for a smooth stop at customs and getting my suitcase before starting on the bus/taxi ride into the city center. I had been forewarned in my travel documents that I would have at least another hour and a half before getting to Tokyo center. A representative from OAT meets me having arranged the transportation. At the very last minute before the bus drives off, he hops onto the bus and informs me in precise English one more time that my stop is first and the driver knows to watch for me.

It isn't until I am in the half-hour taxi ride looking out at the colorful neon display of lights that I have my first inkling how quiet it is everywhere even though the night revelers are out, businessmen in their custom black suits hurry to catch a train and shops are still open. I hardly hear a honking horn, fire truck or loud voice. The taxi driver in his white gloves—steering wheels get sticky in the one hundred percent humidity—keeps his radio volume very low. Speaking of the gloves protocol, it is polite for one driver changing shifts with another to leave a clean wheel. My driver is the first of many who doesn't talk to his passengers; although, I suspect he knows enough English to keep up a conversation. I am soaking in as much as I am able after a thirteen-hour flight from Chicago and appreciate the moments to myself to make my own impressions. Nighttime is a whole different feel to a city than daytime, and I leave it at that.

Arriving at my hotel in a narrow alley around the corner from a main avenue—Japanese use precious land efficiently—after adjusting to following the left hand side of the road traffic, I am greeted almost gushingly by the hotel staff with bowing and nodding—I will write about bowing in the next chapter—and sent on my way to my room.

I am advised ahead that a typical hotel room in Japan is small—space is a premium—and it is a dorm like room. Basic. Organized. The toiletries in the bathroom include all those small items I carry with me everywhere—the toothpaste, toothbrush, shampoo—and a clean cotton kimono and slippers, which I quickly put on. That is the standard practice in every hotel room from one end of the country to the other. The buckwheat pillows in a couple hotel rooms...well, they aren't for me. This small cocoon of a room is rather homey for the four nights I am staying in Tokyo. Of course, there are Westernized hotels, a replica of home, for business people and high-end travelers since those jet-setters pay the premium not to be reminded where they are in the world. Plenty of travelers don't care for the risky business of differences either and are more contented in what they are accustomed to in the States.

There's no energy left in me to explore the room other than getting my computer and phone plugged into the wifi system. I have made the first hurdle successfully. The travel portion sometimes is the roughest part of the entire trip. Mine had started with a cancelled flight at 6:15 am at my home airport, which meant that I missed my connection. When it is my turn at the counter with the airline representative, I calmly state that I am sorry for the problems she must deal with at the end of her shift; however, the airline needs to get me to my destination. It works. She's compassionate. Whew. At bedtime, there isn't any street noise to interrupt me, and before you know it, I am out like a light—lousy pillow, and all.

The next morning after a decent rest on a bed that has a mattress like a board—jet lag is a state of turning your mind to a different time clock—I enter a packed breakfast room and hear nary a sound other than a slight utterance or clicking of a set of chopsticks. Well, I am used to that from travels in other countries for we "ugly Americans" with our self-righteous arrogance is quite a trait that I wish to not be associated with at all. The "ugglies" enter a room and make a big fuss, gather together and let the world know of their presence. That's never been my style, and if I find my voice raising, I quickly cover for it and remind myself I am not in the land of the shouting and free.

I eat in relative silence, in between catching up with my friend traveling from the West Coast—we hadn't seen each other since we met on a trip to Spain last year, decide we are compatible and agree to visit Japan together— and slowly drink roasted green tea, miso soup and assorted slices of smoked fish, rice and vegetables. I leave the corn flakes, the only Western touch on the buffet, alone. That is the first indication that I will be a healthy eater on this vacation, except oh, the saltiness of my daily diet. That is a problem. Japanese people do have high blood pressure, and that must be a factor. I include lots of yogurt and portions of fruit with my Japanese breakfast, though to help with digestion.

My first tour began on a Friday morning after the commuter rush is over, and that's when I perceive the quietness on the daytime streets—everywhere—and at the train terminal, and on trains. Frankly, I am thankful that I have a chance to look around at the huge train station in Tokyo, the first of several transportation centers throughout Japan designed like a city unto itself with floors dedicated to restaurants and shopping. My ears don't hurt from the usual city sounds, and it is a positive feeling of security. I don't know why.

Japanese people speak almost in a whisper, if they speak at all in public places, and I lower my voice considerably to get into the pace of the lifestyle. Children in their school uniforms might be the only exception to break the noise rule as they are gleefully talking with their friends. There is no pushing or shoving. In fact, in the most crowded of situations, Japanese people might nudge, but never push. They know how to maneuver their slight bodies around without physical contact.

In the bustling train terminal where most signs and announcements are limited in English, it isn't hard to at least hear what is spoken, even if it makes no sense to my ears. If I am alone and need help purchasing a ticket, I note ticket agents at information booths, and I am certain I would get assistance. The Japanese pay attention to detail.

There are exceptions of course to the quietness. One is at the Tokyo Metropolitan Central Wholesale Food Market, the largest wholesaler of tuna in the world. It is tricky weaving in and out of the stalls with small equipment moving workers and fish from place to place. In the spirit of the adventure, I partake of a sample of yellow fin tuna sushi—color plays a part in determining the fat proportion of a piece—and naturally, the light pieces—a higher fat content— over a mold of rice lightly braised is mouthwatering. Right then and there, I am a convert to raw sushi and from now on, whenever I am in a city that has fresh fish suppliers, I will order raw—like I will only eat Alaskan wild-caught salmon after a trip there a few years ago. Once you've had the best, nothing else tastes quite right.

A couple days later I am at the busiest cross street in downtown Tokyo at noon while I wait for the light to change. I turn to take a picture of the sea of humanity around me, and I am in a time warp. Surreal. What I am witnessing is all so civilized and calm.

Most trips I have a little uneasiness to deal with before I go to bed each night. It's nothing all that serious usually, and sleep wins over. Not here in Japan. Falling asleep at night is possible as I already am in a peaceful state of mind, and I rest so well tired out from the day's activities. Peace and quiet is prominent and a healthy part of well being in general. Maybe the Japanese have an edge on us.

Looking back on the whole trip, there was no travel stress, or if there were little irritants, I had the ability to keep them from sticking out and jabbing me when I least need to be off my game plan. I thank the quiet atmosphere for that.

Bowing With Grace

Bowing. Everywhere. Daily. I am soon to find out what it all means, and it is not exactly what I had in mind either. To be perfectly honest, before I get up from my rocking chair at home in the spring to start my travels, I read my favorite humorist Dave Barry's book, *Dave Barry Does Japan,* written over twenty years ago and applicable today. My sides split in fits of raucous laughter—all in a polite way—over his impressions of a Japanese cultural more. Oh, how I wish I could be an add-on to the Barry family trip. Is Barry over exaggerating about bowing to make his point? I would see for myself.

Waiting in Chicago for my flight to Tokyo, I use the time for people watching as I customarily do anywhere I am stuck in a packed room. It sure beats hanging out on my cell phone and knowing that everyone within three seats of me will be in on my conversations—Does anyone need to know how I negotiate with the airline to reroute me, or call home for a final good-bye? I am a little more private than that, and I do respect others in public. Cell phones have changed etiquette rules I know, and folks converse wherever or whenever they want to regardless of who might be nearby. I'll go off to a spot to get on the phone far from crying babies and staccato hyperactive voices of salespeople nailing that one last deal before flight time. Nor is it easy to concentrate on a murder mystery that I will save for take-off when my mind can completely let go into back alley scenes and quirky characters stabbing each other in the dark. I'm not much into snacking on airport terminal food either, or hitting the bar out of boredom. Frankly an airport lounge is loud and disruptive, and I am soon to appreciate the quietness in Japan that suits me better.

Just by observing without drawing any attention to myself, those are the "kernels of feed" that I later glean from my "basket" for use in my daily writing. My bi-weekly newspaper column (*the Livingston County News*, Geneseo, NY) calls for fresh material, or my readership will diminish. I can't have that. There's always something to "see" if you really look. First, you have to be still yourself.

Somehow my mind tips me off that there is going to be a new uplifting moment to write about unfolding in front of me while I wait in the Chicago airport. I know it. I'm ready. I remain perfectly still and watch the scene unfold. As the time for boarding comes closer and the Nippon flight attendants—around eighteen of them—gather near the jet way all decked out perfectly in matching light gray suits and carefully polished hair sweeps, I see a business practice that is characteristic of the Japanese, who are known for their efficiency, and there will be examples throughout my visit—queuing lines for train boarding, for example.

The women get in a circle and one "lead" person with a clipboard starts pointing and talking to the others. I am too far away to hear, but I imagine that instructions are given and everyone is clear on their specific assignments. Teamwork is more important than individual accomplishment. The Japanese remain loyal to corporations for life and usually don't change jobs, like in other cultures, hoping to rise to the top for personal gain and wealth. Employees are rewarded well at retirement, too. As soon as the group finishes with their business meeting, they form two parallel lines and from down the hallway the captain and the co-pilot stride through the line with each woman bowing as they pass. It is a formal touch, an art all too forgotten, and I etch that picture in my mind. If everything else is treated as importantly, competency rules and with such care, I will have a lovely time.

An authentic incident of bowing comes on my first full day in Tokyo. For dinner I apparently haven't had my fill of sushi from lunch, and when someone recommends a little neighborhood sushi bar within walking distance of the hotel down a side alley, I am on my way with one of my travel mates. After being greeted by a young male waiter who speaks English fairly well, I permit him to guide me through the menu and make selections. He selects a variety of pieces, and when he returns much later —hand prepared food takes time to create—my tray is laid out like a picture from a cooking magazine. It is a perfect spot to sit, sip a glass of wine and notice people in groups enjoying food and conversation together. And it is quiet, too, with no noisy voices and bar folks yelling at the TV monitor—there is no TV. In fact, the people at the next table turn to us at one point and offer me a sampling of a special crab dish only served at this time of year. You couldn't feel more at home than that anywhere in the world.

When I get up to pay the bill, the waiter shows me a green ceramic tea mug with the business logo—it looks so beautiful in script—and wraps it up as a gift to take home. I am to discover later that any purchase no matter what the price is carefully wrapped in paper and taped like you are a special person. The waiter walks my friend and I out to the sidewalk and bows while thanking us at least ten times—no exaggeration—for coming to the restaurant. As we turn up the street back to the hotel, he is still standing there waving and bowing. He left other diners for a moment to complete the evening for us.

I have the identical experience in other places all over Japan, and I probably should not remain so affected by the first waiter after the pattern continues—no more mugs, though. There is no way that I will ever let that first image in Tokyo at the sushi bar go. I am honored I dined there.

How many times I have wished at other restaurants in unfamiliar places I would feel that way and not leave a stranger. I sort of did in a tapas bar near my hotel in Bilbao, Spain, when I would frequent it during my week's stay for an early dinner—a couple tapas and a glass of Spanish wine—and sit surrounded by locals soaking in the ambiance.

Walking the aisles of department stores while traveling tells me a lot about the lifestyles—clothing for dress occasions to favorite sports teams. I get a chuckle in Kyoto when in the women's intimate section I realize that all the bras for sale are padded A-cups. Oh, well. On the streets in Kamakura I keep seeing brightly designed cotton cloth in small sizes folded in store displays. Napkins? Handkerchiefs? Yes, to both my guesses, and also, my tour guide shows me how gifts are wrapped in the cloth instead of paper. The cloth can then be reused by the recipient for other purposes.

It is impossible not to be bowed to and offered a good morning or evening even if I'm browsing through the selections in a store. Once I make eye contact, the sales person greets me and stops what she is doing. I, on the other hand, suddenly feel like I am appreciated for coming into the establishment. It makes me wonder about the faceless big box stores in America where you never can find help when it is most required, and you learn to fend for yourself. The personal touch is lacking. Not so in Japan.

I do make a purchase, and not one, but three salespersons finalize the sale—one to take my credit card for the transaction, one to box the earrings and a third to be the translator for the others. The oldest department store in Kyoto, Daimaru, will stay in business for another hundred years with courtesies like that; I am convinced.

When I board a crowded commuter train and there isn't an apparent seat, a kindly older gentleman motions for me to have his place. He bows to me. Shouldn't I be thanking him? A lady about my age in a rural restaurant in Gokayama performs a traditional dance after my meal of buckwheat (soba) noodles. She bows to me when I thank her for her original performance before leaving. When leaving Ikuchijima Island, one of the islands of the inland sea, by boat, my server at the local restaurant runs down to the dock and waves goodbye, bows and encircles passengers with a cascade of ribbon we let go as the boat departs.

Sometimes all that bowing can be overkill, and I get tired of it. I don't like the unequal feeling between two human beings. It is great to be appreciated, but effusively treated is not part of my way of handling things. I am uncomfortable bowing back. I wonder if bowing is so ingrained in the Japanese that it really doesn't mean anything and I am making a bigger deal out of it than is necessary? Let the doorman bow. When the policeman bows after he motions me forward to cross the street and the ticket taker at the temple nods like a robot individually to a steady stream of hundreds of visitors, I accept it.

I have to understand this cultural symbol, and my tour guide explains that the Japanese people have serious self-esteem problems making them submissive and ultra-polite. With a high national suicide rate, the Japanese struggle to achieve self-worth. Americans grow up with egos, hold on tenaciously to their individual rights, and are not lacking in self-serving ways, if not down right arrogant stances. The Japanese, on the other hand, have a group mindset and tend to trust those in authority—teachers, rulers —and do not question for that is considered rude. I am thinking about the evening I went into a fine restaurant and instead of making my selection from the menu, and perhaps a substitution or two, I trust the chef to cook his best meal for me in one of the three price ranges I select. The suffering the Japanese faced during the long years of World War II because the groupthink of the military deemed it valuable to start a war with the United States—and recognizing the need for it to end— leaves all the people hoping for peace. Japanese folks place a lot of shame on themselves, from making sure that their cars are new and spotless at all times to keeping their homes neat and tidy. On a motor coach heading to Hakone in stop and go traffic, I pick up on the car situation. That inner monitoring has its positive and negative points.

The Japanese people demand high expectations on themselves to achieve and honor other human beings for the good of the group. It goes way beyond treating tourists well; although, they are high on the list in acing that feat. It is part of their way of life. Living on an isolated island without a constant flow of immigrants, their society is pure and sticks to its past social mores.

A friend stationed in Japan over fifty years ago in the Air Force is a bit taken back that politeness still rules. He thought that Westernized movies and culture would have taken hold of the younger generations. That says something about cultural values and how parental training insists upon them.

The United States, on the other hand, is a "melting pot" and diversity is part of the culture of a huge nation. That intrigues me, and I am open to the acceptance of others, which makes my nation rich in so many ways. Pride in our country is a trait that I feel is either overboard, or non-existent with our population. There doesn't appear to be a balance between patriotism and apathy.

I am being rather simplistic here. There are many Japanese artists, designers and architects who think outside the box and have not bought into the rigid system. They survive and go on to flourish artistically on an international level.

Good will comes from being in Japan during April and May. It reminds me to slow down, show kindness to strangers and be open to "paying it forward," frequently more as a habit than a spur of the moment decision. Returning home via San Francisco airport, the salesperson at the coffee counter never so much as gives me eye contact. I thank her twice after waiting extra long for my cup without criticism in my voice. Evidently, she could care less, and I am invisible once again in society.

High achievement is important to me, and I put forth my foremost effort naturally to succeed. With that can come selfishness, jealousy and shoving others out of the way if I am not careful in monitoring my attitude. A personal best is what you strive for without forgetting that life is a team sport.

It is humbling to observe that in a Japanese mindset there is respect for other people.

Finding My Way

After several days of intense sightseeing in Tokyo, it is time to spend a couple in Hakone, a popular resort area about 50 miles west of the city for a different glimpse of Japan. The motor coach speeds on smooth two lane highways passing small streams and rice paddies before getting into more mountainous terrain. The natural sunlight gives way to miles or so of long tunnels as the bus ascends on narrower roads. There's a lot of traffic for Golden Week celebrations, and I look down from my perch at what passengers do—video gaming on hand held devices. That sounds about right.

First, I will explore the might and majesty of Mount Fuji, the highest mountain peak in Japan at 3,776.24 m (12,389 ft, an active stratovolcano that last erupted in 1707–08.) It lies about 100 kilometers (60 mi) southwest of Tokyo and can be seen from there on a clear day. Mount Fuji's exceptionally symmetrical cone, which is snow-capped several months a year, is a well-known symbol of Japan and it is frequently depicted in art and photographs, as well as visited by sightseers and climbers.

Mount Fuji is in full view—I am in luck—in spite of the fact that the day is windy and cloudy with major rain anticipated by evening. The mountain is divided into 10 stations, or levels, and today I will ascend halfway up by bus to take in some breathtaking panoramas.

The road up the final curves hums a tune—there's a steady beat to the intervals of bumps—and I sing a traditional song: *Sticking out the peak from the clouds, Overlooking all surrounding mountains, King of Thunder is roaring way down below, Fuji is the No. 1 mountain in Japan.*

The snow at the summit makes me shiver, and I quickly throw on a red fleece jacket before hopping off the bus. The wind is picking up, sprinkles of rain spot my face, and I hold onto my hat trying to get a couple photos in almost impossible conditions. It's not worth the agony and the reminder that I just left winter behind a few weeks ago. I blow into the small post office and send a postcard home, though, and admire the awesome sight out the window.

I don't know it presently, but tomorrow will be an absolutely gorgeous day of viewing from another location on the water. I am one of the fortunate visitors for Mount Fuji only shows its face about once a month, and I will have two in a row. That same thing happened when I visited Denali in Alaska. Where's the third mountain for me? Kilimanjaro?

At the resort in Hakone I prepare for a banquet meal by putting on my blue and gray yukata and sandals, an outfit that I wear at every meal with only my undergarments for the next couple days. The rest of the Japanese guests are dressed identically, and I marvel at how freeing I am in public in my kimono going through the breakfast line looking over the spread not having to fret about my waistband tightening for every day on the road. Each of us ties the front bow differently as there is no set way, and other than that, I am one of many novice yukata wearers trying to keep flowing sleeves out of the food at the table. Don't laugh. It's not so easy.

If you are wondering what a Japanese style banquet meal might consist of in courses, let me give you the menu for my first night in Hakone:

Small Cup Starter: Avocado Salad dressed tofu on rice cake wafer with shitake, jelly and azuki beans
Hors d'oeuvre: Marinated mallard duck and red onions
Sashimi: Assorted local raw fish of the season

Grilled fish: Grilled sablefish with Saikyo miso on eggplant
Main dish: Fritters of soy marinated bonito
Food boiled: Conger eel, broad beans, brocken, wheat bran, thin omelet
Pot: Shabu-shabu (thin slices of beef parboiled in hot soup with carrot, mustard, spring noodles and onions added)
Soup: Red miso soup
Dessert: Miso pudding

It sounds like a lot of food, but small portions prevail and that combines for a balanced meal.

As for the hot spring (onsen) in the hotel, I study from an informative paper handed me on the proper way to enter and take part in the public one—by sex—or use the Western-style private stall. You must take off all your clothes in the changing room, and place them in a basket together with your bath towel. Japanese hot springs are enjoyed naked and swimsuits are not allowed. Unfortunately, that's as far as I go with the experience. It is 40-44 degrees C (104-108 degrees F), and I am woozy from way too much heat. Alas, it is not meant for my body at my age.

If I were to continue further, I would rinse my body with water from the tap, enter the bath and soak for a while. After leaving the bath, I'd wash my body with soap and water at the tap while sitting on a stool. Soap and shampoo are provided but not allowed in the bath water. I'd tidy up my space after I am finished, re-enter the bath and soak more to get the full affect of the minerals on my body. I do not rinse this time. I did get reports from a few of my fellow travelers that they had a sensational bath.

Younger Americans who have fewer inhibitions about how they dress in public, would no doubt have the same reaction to naked public baths and wearing loose kimonos schlepping around a hotel lobby in Japan. It's a different cultural norm here.

Mesmerized, looking out my window after a very early thunderstorm booming and reverberating off the mountain walls, I watch the fog stream pass by and write a traditional haiku verse of 5-7-5 syllables in praise of nature's harmony.

Fog weaves a ribbon
Through Japanese cedar trees
Tying earth to sky.

The Japanese had a longstanding love for poetry predating the haiku form. As early as the 7th century, Japanese narrative poetry included short lyrical poems. Gods burst forth into song or poem and these works are carried down by oral tradition. Japanese brains are tuned to nature and allow lots of room for playfulness.

I am unaware that below me in the courtyard is another example of a gorgeous Japanese garden that will show off its glory when the sun comes out in a couple hours. I am reminded of the many serious photographers and gardeners that I know, and how they would have a field day admiring the shapes and arrangements pruned just so meticulously for one aesthetic reason—simplicity. Ornamental Japanese maples are pruned to arch in certain directions and they are propped by bamboo poles to hold them firmly if necessary.

The Japanese garden is more than just for viewing, however. One participates in the moment. The small bridge found in most gardens, like the one in Hakone, is a pathway to paradise with a clear religious message. The garden leads viewers into a meditative state and is a cultural treasure reminding one of the impermanence of people and things.

"Participating" is something Westerners are familiar with at amusement parks, but not so much with gardens. People are not drawn into the harmony and calmness for those are two different states of mind in Eastern philosophy not universally acknowledged in the West.

It is here while in Hakone that I work my method of figuring out how to quickly find the proper change in my purse. Two of the coins have holes in the center. Those come from China originally. Before the days of paper money, people carried a lot of coins with them, so they found it convenient to make holes in the middle and join them all together with strings like the beads on a necklace. Today, the holes in the coins serve a new purpose. The holes assist blind people. By feeling the ridges in the edges of the coins and the holes in the middle, they can tell which is which. It is also helpful to a stranger to the yen, too, like me, finding the 5 and 50 cents quickly.

Another thoughtful courtesy in Japan is the narrow yellowed grooved strips about a foot in diameter on sidewalks and in public train stations allowing blind people to function independently.

I have no problem in a convenience store picking up a bottle of water and opening up my change purse letting the cashier pick out the coins for the transaction. Often there is a line of customers behind me, and I feel embarrassed to hold everyone up. However, I never sense any "waiting in line" rage and just patient people. Japan is indeed an ideal learning place while I find my way.

With paper money I move the decimal point over two places to the left, and 10,000 yen becomes 100 dollars. I use more cash than I regularly do traveling and save my credit card for bigger expenses. In restaurants if you tell your server you are using a card, or even not, the bill comes separated by guest.

For the big conversions I love the app I have on my phone to do number crunching for me. There is no tipping in Japan and that makes dining out and taking a taxi less complicated. My tour guide makes clear that going to either a bank or ATM at a Seven Eleven— yes, they're in Japan along with Kentucky Fried Chicken, MacDonald's and you name it—works for our American cards. As much as Japan is relatively safe with a low crime rate, I find it wise to use the same precautions I would anywhere else carrying a small sum of bills.

I haven't found an English speaking TV network yet, and in its place I watch endless Japanese infomercials selling women's facial and body creams. Japanese women look ten years younger as their skin doesn't wrinkle, and part of that is attributed to using hats and umbrellas—and this magical cream, too. In a department store in Hiroshima I discover one whole floor exclusively for umbrellas in every size and color imaginable, and figure that every Japanese woman owns at least two or three. A traveler from Oregon tells me that she has a fetish for raincoats for coping with duck soup weather, and she understands perfectly well why Japanese ladies would collect umbrellas. My tour guide wears cut-off gloves to cover the backs of her hands, too, and she is not the only one on the streets. Women are sensitive to how their age can be detected by looking at their hands. She uses the cream, too, and points it out to me on a shelf in a store. "Try it," she insists, and I put a dab on my hands rubbing it in letting the gold leaf added in to sparkle when I move my hands.

Also on TV, there is an abundance of silly quiz shows with high-pitched giggling a mile a minute, two melodramatic soap operas—more giggling—and adult cartoons. Anime is Japanese hand-drawn or computer animation. This term applies to all animation often characterized by colorful graphics, vibrant characters and fantastical themes—along with a news station. At a couple hotels I am able to get the BBC in English, and it is a delightful change—up to a point. I decide it is just as well to do without the news—my news app informs me of major events—and relax.

I take a couple walks—one canopied by Japanese cedar trees in Hakone, and the other in a bamboo jungle as high as the sky later in the trip—and I exercise my legs and examine what's around me. What I require in my travels is a tour that allows down time to meander and pursue my own interests. I do have a lot to consider before it gets lost deeply in my brain never to appear again. The best highlights come in the most unexpected places, and while nothing crops up on these walks, they are refreshing respites from a day's group activities.

In Hakone the cherry trees are in blossom around the town, and it is a sight to behold—thick clusters of delicately muted pinks and whites. I don't realize there is a purpose in where the trees are placed. Most Japanese schools and public buildings have cherry blossom trees outside of them. Since the fiscal and school year both begin in April, in many parts of the country, the first day of work or school coincides with the cherry blossom season.

In Japan, cherry blossoms symbolize clouds due to their nature of blooming en masse, besides being an enduring metaphor for the ephemeral nature of life, an aspect of Japanese cultural tradition that is often associated with Buddhist influence. "Hanami" is the centuries-old practice of picnicking and drinking sake under a blooming cherry blossom tree during festival time.

During World War II, the cherry blossom was used to motivate the Japanese people, to stoke nationalism and militarism among the populace. Even prior to the war, they were used in propaganda to inspire "Japanese spirit," as in the "Song of Young Japan," exulting in "warriors" who were "ready like the myriad cherry blossoms to scatter."

As I explore Japan first hand, I am reminded that the tension between periods of isolationism and globalization has had a tremendous influence Japanese culture—visual arts, theatre, architecture and film. Myths and stories of the gods are fused into the belief system of the people along with a major portion of superstition.

Every time I walk past a newsstand, there is someone pouring over a manga, a comic book created in Japan in the 19th century. In Japan, people of all ages read manga. The medium includes works in a broad range of genres: action-adventure, business/commerce, comedy, detective, historical drama, horror, mystery, romance, science fiction and fantasy, sexuality, sports and games, and suspense, among others. I pick one up and note its intricate pen and ink drawings showing action lifting off the page.

It is not many days into my trip before I am more than satisfied with all things Japanese, and the deeper I let myself invest into each moment, the more peaceful I am. I believe I have slowed down appropriately.

Rural Life and Beyond

I have been waiting for time to spend in mountain villages, and on a misty, foggy Sunday morning the weather provides an interesting backdrop to Shirakawa-go and Gokayama, Japan's two UNESCO World Heritage Sites located in the Shogawa river valley in central Japan.

A hardy rain fell the night before. To me, there is something about the blurry vistas smudged in cloud cover that heightens my awareness of what is hiding behind nature's draperies after a storm. Not sure of the wildlife in the area, I keep alert to any possibility. Alas, it is sleepy time in the hills and valleys, and I am left alone. Not even a resident is outside to disturb my peace. It is a delightful hour to drop trivial notions and see what unfolds on its own.

Because of their relative isolation, these areas have developed independently of Japanese society, resulting in their unique culture and lifestyle. It has been a medieval way of life until quite recently. Some might say that these people haven't missed anything in such a pastoral setting free of fast paced living. Certainly it makes for a thoughtful visit, and like I do in other settings, I wonder if I would be suited for such life.

In addition to creating their own dances, festivals and traditions, residents developed a distinctive architectural style known as gassho. Characterized by steeply pitched thatched roofs—about 60 degrees—forming a nearly equilateral triangle that are both striking and elegant, these dwellings are considered to be some of the most efficient farmhouses in Japan. A docent reveals that gassho is originally a Buddhist hand symbol that is made by pressing together the palms and ten fingers in front of one's chest and is evoked by believers whenever they are worshipping Buddha. Picture the shape of a gassho-style roof, and the image makes sense.

The house that I visit is four stories in one part and a section that is five. Silk worms were raised on the third floor and above. Those floors are shorter so that in the past the silk worms could be fed mulberry leaves within easy reach. I climb up ladders crouching to observe the empty space. The attic is divided for many purposes. Up until 1910, a large extended family of about thirty-five members lived and worked together under the control of the head of the household. Presently, there are six people living in the house.

Most of these homes are 100 to 200 years old and are on the World Heritage List. The enormous roof is supported by stout oak beams called chonabari, which are curved at the base. These beams come from trees grown on the mountainside and develop the curve naturally. No nails are used. The roof frame is lashed together with rope and twisted hazel boughs, called neso. Today, these homes are kept up and maintained by a collective group of people in an owner's cooperative. Each side of a thatched roof house is re-thatched every 25 years as a group project.

The gasho style is very rational, having a strong structural design that enables them to survive in harsh conditions created by deep snow. At the same time, it is spacious for living and working. I am impressed with Japanese building techniques: another example of how time invested wisely during planning and utilizing nearby resources pays off in well-built structures.

While I am served tea on the first floor, costumed dancers performing an ancient dance called, Dengaku, entertain in flowing orange outfits. This folk music was performed during the time of rice planting, and then later, introduced to the imperial court. I am fascinated watching the dancers each holding a pair of bamboo sticks, a musical instrument called a kokiriko, made from spliced bamboo and knotted pieces—108 wooden pieces joined. The particular choice of a number of sticks represents protection for the 108 worldly desires of Buddhism. The music is both melancholy and haunting in its tune with a resonance of innocence and simplicity from an earlier age.

Before I leave in the afternoon, though, the sun is out and there is an entirely new look to the place—more immediate and detailed. I finish up outside walking a path, and sometimes it is on a board laid over a marshy area near a rice paddy. A middle-aged woman in a tunic and dark pants using a hoe stoops over a field of wheat exactly like her forefathers must have done. She pauses to look up at me, and goes back to work. There is more to be done before nightfall, I assume, from where she is standing in the middle of the plot. Further along, a man in a modern red tractor with large treads on the tires drives into a rice paddy to move the earth around and stimulate the crop.

I make my own paper with members of the local community in their workshop using the ancient methods of boiling, cleansing, beating the fiber to loosen it. Ideally, it would be a slow process, except the craftspeople speed it up to complete the demonstration. Washi paper, I am told, has existed for over 1200 years when 400 official documents were presented to the imperial court. I am bringing home a brightly colored journal for my personal notes as a remembrance of the day here. My cream and red journal may not be filled with royal edicts and decrees; however, it will hold precious words and phrases vital to my writing.

It is on to watch women in the community center make rice-cakes using methods that have stood the test of time. I am invited to use the heavy mallet to pound the mixture in a giant vat, and one or two swings are enough to get the idea of this labor-intensive recipe. The final product...well, it tastes like a lump of glue going down by throat. With a few sips of green tea, my stomach only rumbles a few times. Lunch is due shortly.

Visiting in a mountain community urges me to appreciate how important it is to not lose sight of one's heritage. It is an absolute pleasure spending a day in a living museum putting my hands and mind to work.

Bullet Trains, Shoes and Miso Soup

Little do I know that one of my favorite activities is traveling on a bullet train, the legendary high-speed train service pioneered by the Japanese. The Japanese call this quick transit train the shinkansen, and its speed at times is up to 200 mph.

I feel like I am a kid again. My tour guide forewarns me that the train stops only for a minute to let passengers on and off, and I must stand at the precise location to enter the reserved coach with my seat assignment showing on the ticket. Sure enough, the train halts and people exit orderly, and I rush to get my wheeled carry on and myself in, too, without pushing or shoving. I don't realize as the train starts up so smoothly—there is no clickty-clack of railroad tracks and swaying from side-to-side—that I am still walking the aisle and putting my suitcase in the overhead rack when the train is out of the station. My seat is spacious with lot of legroom to stretch out. Looking out the window at an object far off in the distance helps from getting a little dizzy. Today, on a bullet train to Nagoya before transferring to an express train to Kanazawa, I have lunch in the Japanese style—I purchased a packed lunch called eki-ben at the station to enjoy on the train. It's not long after that when I fall asleep. Trains do that, you know.

Several times while riding the bullet train I think that it is a shame that our infrastructure is crumbling at home, or otherwise the bullet train would be an efficient alternative to planes and cars. Japan continues to improve on its mass transportation system in the meantime; although, an individual ticket is not cheap on a bullet train. The other people in the car are daily commuters and travelers, too. Backpackers and Europeans with small pieces of luggage, all comfortable with rail travel, navigate Japan rather easily.

My last bullet train ride is from Hiroshima to a stop close to Kensai International Airport where I transfer to an express line through a long underground tunnel. Kensai airport is famous for it is located on an artificial island of reclaimed land in the middle of Osaka Bay, the first of its kind in the world. Think about it: No one in the neighborhood is disturbed by airplane noise. Landing and taking off is quite the thrill here, and I am the one looking from both windows.

Probably the least favorite thing that I have to do in Japan is removing my shoes. I am told in my pre-travel packet to bring slip on shoes along with sneakers as some days between temples, restaurants and homes my shoes are off more than on.

Taking off my shoes is not the problem. The proper way to observe this etiquette is not a natural habit at first. I want to respect my hosts and honor the tradition, though, and I learn the procedure and pull it off with only a few unnoticeable slipups.

Mrs. Janko Osada invites me to her home for tea and a little light conversation. The visit is arranged through my tour company, and when the taxi lets me out on a quiet residential street, she is by the door welcoming me. It is my chance to ask a woman of near my age questions about daily life. Mrs. Osada is dressed in a kimono with her sleek black hair pulled back in a bun. Later on she explains that as soon as I leave, she will put on her Western clothes again. She wears her traditional outfit for entertaining guests.

First, I have to remove my shoes. The main entrance of a Japanese house is called a genkan, a foyer-like room where I take off my shoes and step up into the home. The actual line between inside and outside is not the front door. In Japan, the line between inside and outside is the step that is built into the genkan floor. The genkan has two sections: the ground level area beside the door and the elevated area that is level with the house's first floor. The lower area is usually paved in flagstone or concrete. The upper area, which is considered to be an interior living space, has a wooden or tatami-mat floor.

In regard to shoes, each of the two areas has an etiquette: No street shoes are permitted on the upper level, and no stocking feet or bare feet are permitted on the lower level. Mrs. Osada says that in a Japanese person's mind, this system keeps the floor of the home free of outside dirt. It also prevents the bottom of my socks from becoming dirty, which is important because my socks inevitably come in direct contact with interior floors.

So, what do I actually do when Mrs. Osada opens the door and greets me? I step out of one shoe, place my socked foot on the upper area and while balancing myself, slip out of the second shoe. When both feet are on the upper level I am ready to visit. I bend down and turn my shoes around facing the front door. I am careful to avoid stepping on the edges of the tatami mat walking into the dining room. The more I perform this piece of etiquette, and quickly too, it becomes a little more like a routine.

Mrs. Osada leads me into a dining room area around a low table, motions for me to sit down on a fluffy cushion and she explains that she teaches ikebana classes, the art of floral arranging, to her students here. More than simply putting flowers in a container, ikebana is a disciplined art form in which nature and humanity are brought together. Contrary to the idea of floral arrangement as a collection of particolored or multicolored arrangement of blooms, ikebana often emphasizes other areas of the plant, such as its stems and leaves, and draws emphasis toward shape, line and form. Though ikebana is a creative expression, it has certain rules governing its form. The artist's intention behind each arrangement is shown through a piece's color combinations, natural shapes, graceful lines, and the usually implied meaning of the arrangement. Her English is quite fluent, and with the help of the translator on her laptop, she and I get by while I ask about her classes. She shows me an arrangement that she had just made from flowers from the florist; however, sometimes she can use what's in her garden. She pulls it apart and then demonstrates the placement of each flower. She insists that I try for myself, and one by one, I place each stem in the container in a certain position and for its height according to her plan. We laugh over my meager attempt. It takes a practiced eye and skill working with both low, shallow containers and tall cylindrical vases. Originally, ikebana developed from the Buddhist ritual of offering flowers to the spirits of the dead. I think I woke some of the restless ones up this morning.

Mrs. Osada's husband is not at home this morning as he is out training for a triathlon meet coming soon. Her adult children and grandchildren will be coming later to visit—it's Mother's Day—with flowers and candy, favorites of Japanese moms. She shows me their pictures as we visit other rooms in her two-story house in a suburban area outside Kamazawa, a city not bombed during WWII.

When it is time to leave Mrs. Osada's, I step directly into my shoes without standing on the ground in my stocking feet. She asks the taxi driver to take our picture, and she runs inside to print it out for me. Japanese people are not verbose outwardly in their visits with company; instead, they are polite and restrained as is Mrs. Osada.

When I visit in some Western homes in the States, family members and guests remove their shoes before entering. However, without a clear line separating inside and out, stocking clad guests can end up standing in a dirty foyer, with shoes piles up in an unsightly mess. Other homes are designed in an Eastern tradition like the Japanese.

The Japanese appreciate a way of life that is fragile—cherry blossoms are in bloom only a short time—and like the cycle of nature, flower arrangements connect the ground to the sky in a delicate, pleasing manner for a brief moment. Westerners tend to cling to people and natural cycles without letting go comfortably. It's a control issue that they fight over internally that the Japanese do not understand.

My ongoing love of miso soup—a traditional Japanese soup consisting of a stock called "dashi" into which softened miso paste is mixed—never disappoints, and from place to place it is my ritual. Varying ingredients are added depending on regional and seasonal recipes. No one mentions to me the proper time during a meal to have soup, and often I save it until the end when it has cooled down. My tour guide eats three or more bowls of miso soup every day as it possibly cuts a woman's risk of developing breast cancer according to her knowledge. Miso soups also tend to be low in calories, but are filling because of the high protein content.

I watch and learn proper etiquette one lesson at a time during my visit. It is bad manners to hold your chopsticks over the food on the table while you think about what to eat next. No licking them, sticking them with food, pulling dishes with them, or placing them on top of plates. When I become more proficient with chopsticks, I use them as tweezers for picking up, tearing and cutting, too.

In a Japanese home each person has his or her own set of chopsticks. I find an artisan's shop by pure accident that makes hand engraved chopsticks and his son proudly sells me a matched pair in dusty pink and mauve designs on dark wood. I regret that I didn't ask the kind of wood his father used.

The most prevalent material used to make chopsticks is aspen wood. Aspen is used to make the disposable chopsticks used in restaurants. About 20 billion pair are used yearly, mostly in Japan. Many other materials are used to make chopsticks designed for more than one use. Metal chopsticks are common in some areas, and elaborate chopsticks may be carved of precious materials such as ivory or jade. Most chopsticks are made of some variety of wood, and coated with oil, paint, or lacquer. Some varieties of chopstick wood have superstitions related to them. For example, chestnut chopsticks are said to bring wealth and black persimmon chopsticks, long life. Other typical woods used for chopsticks are pine, cedar, cherry, sandalwood and paulownia. A traditional Japanese material is a sandwich of thin boards of maple, pine, and cedar called shuboku wood. In general, the wood used needs to be relatively hard and impervious to water. The color and grain of the wood is also important for fine quality chopsticks.

White rice is a staple of the Japanese diet, and there is rice on every buffet table and with each meal. My tour guide cautions me to eat everything else on the plate first, and if my stomach still doesn't feel full, then go for the carbohydrate. She avoids rice entirely keeping her petit figure perfectly shaped. When I do hit the scale after returning home, I am quite happy than I gained only a couple pounds.

For some reason the Japanese get a kick out of fried chicken, and they have their own take on this American dish. I try chicken, but much prefer tempura, a Japanese dish of seafood or vegetables that is battered and deep fried. Besides, the portions are large and easy to grasp with chopsticks without making a mess on the table. I read in a brochure that on Christmas Day Japanese families go to Kentucky Fried Chicken restaurants for a meal, which is amusing to me.

Eating out in the evenings I watch for how Japanese families dine. Of course, they do it quietly, too. Before a meal, many Japanese people put their hands together in a gesture, which looks like a Christian prayer. It comes from an old Buddhist action called gassho. People say, Itadakimasu, which is a humble expression that means, "I will receive." Although it appears the same as the Christian prayer gesture, Japanese people are not thanking God. They are just expressing a general feeling of thankfulness to nature for the food that they are going to eat.

I do go to a sake factory for a flight of several selections, and sample them along with plum wine. The wine I much prefer as a taste for sake is not one I have acquired.

Many in my group drink local Japanese beer throughout the trip and are quite complimentary in their reviews. I stick with imported wine – red and white – and one particular Riesling from Germany stands out with the crispness for my palate.

One night in Kyoto after a satisfying meal, I am wandering around the gourmet food section of the department store with a friend, and we notice an ice cream stand advertising in English brown rice ice cream. I'm usually up for anything—even octopus and squid sushi—and I buy a cone. The girl at the counter tells me that I must put soy sauce over it, and boy, does that bring out the flavor. Who would have thought? There are a couple other bottles on the counter, and my friend lifts one up to inspect before the girl runs over from the counter exclaiming, "No, no, not for pouring on your ice cream. That's salad dressing." We all get a good laugh over saving her ice cream in the nick of time. It's always the little memories that linger long after the trip is finished.

Environmental Cleanliness Rules

It is appalling watching our highways and public places spill over with trash needlessly from citizens who do not value their environment. There are so many times when I am out walking in the country on back roads that I come across plastic bags entangled in tree branches, dented beer cans and leftover taco lunches spilling from paper bags on the edges of the road tossed by a lazy careless person probably thinking, "It's not my spot. Who cares?" Well, some of us—and there are plenty of like-minded souls—take tremendous pride in where we live and want to preserve it for future generations. Unfortunately, to keep my wits about me, I have to look the other way; otherwise, my moment for relaxation is gone. Routinely, I do go through our property edges—you are in for it worse living on a corner—and pick up my acres.

It's the way I was brought up, and I have a bit of internal shame that would slap me if I were to carelessly litter the earth. My parents taught me well, and I don't have to hear their voices. I pick up my space wherever I am and leave it better than I found it in some cases. What makes someone else, on the other hand, think so differently is beyond me. I am sad and angry all at the same time. With a little extra effort…what would it take to get Americans to change gears and make cleanliness a daily routine?

I follow the sage words of Wendell Berry, an activist, writer and environmentalist, and hold his thoughts close to my heart:

> We have lived our lives by the assumption that what was good for us would be good for the world. We have been wrong. We must change our lives so that it will be possible to live by the contrary assumption, that what is good for the world will be good for us. And that requires that we make the effort to know the world and learn what is good for it.

It is a roundabout way to get at the point for writing about the high praise that I offer Japanese society, for theirs is an exceptionally neat and efficient country. Cleanliness is a way of life. It certainly is a pleasure co-existing with them for a short while, too. Considering that a humongous number of people reside in such a small area, it stands to reason that organization rules.

One sweltering afternoon in Arashiyama after touring two beautiful gardens—Zen gardens with huge ponds, elevated rock groupings and delicately pruned trees—it is time for a green tea ice cream cone break. I find a stand along the street, purchase my cone and sit with the moment in sheer ecstasy. The cool ice cream sides down my throat. I am becoming infused with green tea for breakfast, lunch and dinner, and it is early in the trip.

The dilemma comes when I can't find a trash bin—you don't find trash receptacles often in public places in Japan—to drop the paper wrapper around the cone. I go back to the girl at the ice cream stand. She can hardly speak English and really doesn't understand when I show her the paper wrinkled in my hand. I assume that there is a trashcan in her workstation and look behind her. There is one, but she doesn't offer to take my trash. I end up folding the paper and slipping it in my purse to discard in my hotel room. Maybe there is a bit of inconvenience involved, but I didn't suffer any.

Realistically, in the big and smaller cities, trash dumpsters are evident if you glance down back or side alleys. None ever appear overflowing, and the smell of garage does not permeate the air like in other cities when the thermometer goes up. What's the secret?

Clean walls and streets are prominent. I think back to the evening that my plane landed in Tokyo. It has been occupied for the last thirteen hours, and there isn't a scrap of paper on the floor when I walk up the aisle. I do recall the flight attendants collecting trash after meals, but I don't believe they made a "last appeal" as the plane is getting ready to land. Seemingly, the work had been done. I hope I remembered to fold my used blanket and that I didn't leave it in a heap on the seat or floor.

It doesn't take more than one morning on public transportation in Tokyo to notice there is no graffiti or wall art and not a scrap of litter anywhere. How refreshing. I feel it is also a sad commentary on what I am confronted with at home.

In European countries wall art is an acceptable form of free expression, and I amble the streets of Madrid and Barcelona where apartment doors are uniquely decorated to personalize an otherwise dark and bland wall. I will admit that I find it interesting and often amusing to see how people express themselves in a swirl of art. The Japanese do not think as a group in that vein, though. They personify a society with a balanced and uncluttered feel to architecture, design and beauty.

Once in a public garden early in the morning, I watch the cleaning crew in dark blue work clothes with typical Chinese sun hats sorting and cleaning the pebbles on the paths with wooden brooms and scooping containers. It is a simple and mundane task that they perform every single day.

Rice paddies cultivated by men or women wading in deep boots and using rakes to skim the water checking the plants has been done in the same way for centuries, or now, by a modern tractor, where each section is neat and orderly. Every inch of squared space is used around a home or building with nothing wasted. For some reason I have pictured in my mind rice paddies further away from homes, and in a location you had to walk to for work. Not so in reality.

Many countries have a plastic bag ban, and Japan is one of them, except in the touristy areas. In department store basement gourmet food aisles to fish markets, customers bring their own colorful bags. It's a habit, and for commuters in a city, it limits how much you purchase at one time.

Very rarely are paper napkins available in a Japanese restaurant. You do receive a warmed white towel about the size of a washcloth for wiping your hands throughout the meal. Accustomed to spreading a napkin over my lap, it takes careful eating to keep my precious travel clothes clean. Ramen noodle soup is a perfect example. You have to get it right with the slurping like a native, or your clothes are covered. I watch diners in one restaurant, and they pull up a cluster of noodles with chopsticks before taking the bowl in both hands to sip the liquid. There doesn't appear to be any proper way, and I learn to put my bowl up to my mouth for less noodle dribbling.

At heavily visited temples and shrines, the grounds and buildings are immaculate. Considering all the throngs of people wandering through—tons of school children on field trips—I focus on the ornate building design and history of them, instead of being annoyed at messy unkempt areas.

Speaking of school field trips, my tour guide doesn't understand my question when I ask if it is acceptable in Japan for teachers to bring children to religious shrines. I explain how in my country that is a clear separation of church and state—it is in Japan, too—and locally in a school district students study religion from an historical aspect; although, taking an educational field trip to a place of worship would never happen. Her reply to me basically said that in Japan people are tolerant and honor religion without interference from those advocating political correctness.

Public restrooms—only a few squat type toilets are left, thank goodness—are immaculate and often do not have paper towel dispensers, or hand dryers. Drip dry is the modus of operation, and every traveler knows to carry hand sanitizing liquid and Kleenex for just those places. The Japanese are ingenious with heated toilet seats, too. I come to adore them and think how inviting the first thing in the morning on a freezing day to have that luxury at home. Ah.

Anyone that knows me wouldn't classify me as a neat freak. I am not to the other extreme either. Basically, I am a happy middle-of-the-roader. It does offend me that thoughtlessness overweighs cleanliness, though. I applaud the Japanese.

Dumplings, Brooklyn Pizza and Tofu

The young waitress hands a menu all in Japanese to my friend and I in a restaurant specializing in dumplings, and we take a long glance over it unable to decipher a single word. Not to worry. We are in the midst of a new adventure. Being in this very position has happened numerous times in the past on other trips, and we decide to sit back letting things work itself out. They usually do, too, and with a story to tell at home.

We figure the dumpling part out by looking at the plastic samples of the food in the window display before coming into the restaurant. Granted, I am aware that travel guides tell you to stay away from restaurants that show pictures as those restaurants are not authentic ones for a true cultural experience. I agree. It's like putting out a sign, "tourists welcome." In this particular case, it is an exception to the rule and as authentic as you will find.

There are several clues that we are going to be in for a real home cooked meal. The place is tiny and as we walk in and choose one of the four tables, the owner gets up from his newspaper and—seriously, I am not kidding—he put on his chef's apron and hat. The sole waitress is probably his round-faced teenage daughter slightly on the heavy side herself, quite unusual in the older Japanese population. Like other younger Japanese, American fast food restaurants are doing their number on weight issues in Japan. She leaves her stack of schoolbooks behind the front counter and comes out to greet us with a bow. The only problem is that neither father nor daughter speak one word of English. That's where I am grateful for the pictures, and somehow by making a guess and pointing, my friend and I order four large assorted dumplings—one of each filled with pork, shrimp, vegetables and chicken.

At least that's what we think we will get on our plates. I've been in other countries where the waiter brings a meal totally unplanned for—a minor shock—and I muddle through with a laugh like the plate overflowing with a large portion of haggis in Scotland when I believe it will be a sampler plate with other regional foods. Or, the sausage in Austria that is smothered in gravy and the beef hearts in Germany. I'm not one to offend or ask for a different menu item, and I will grin and eat whatever is in front of me.

A second clue leading me to rest assured that we have an excellent place to eat is that we have a decent wait time for our meal, and we watch the chef prep—lots of chopping with his big knife—and steam. Our waitress goes back to her homework, and my friend and I drink our wine and beer in no hurry.

When the dumplings arrive in a steamer basket, they are plump with steam coming off in spirals of heat. One bite after they cool down, and we are in for a unique meal. All four are flavorful in separate ways, and I can't pick a favorite.

What I appreciate about international dining is that you are never rushed to finish so that a new group of people can use your seat. A meal is to be savored with a drink or two between good friends. When it is time to pay our bill, the waitress has nicely divided it for us. She bows very pleased apparently when she takes away our cleaned plates. Perhaps, she understands English a little bit better than we give her credit, and she is simply shy. We attempt finding the right words so that she can share with her father that we thought he makes fine dumplings.

The dumpling restaurant is one example of a collection of establishments on a single floor dedicated to food in train stations, shopping malls and department stores. Usually, my friend and I circle through to see all the possibilities, then one or the other of us makes a decision. It always leads to a delicious meal, and we go for our gut feelings when a place seems right for us. Most restaurants aren't that full, so we can never judge it solely by that factor either. There aren't many tourists, and it is primarily Japanese people. At home in an ethnic restaurant, I am fairly certain when I see others of a similar culture eating with family and friends, that I have found a better than average place.

I feel the most conspicuous and out-of-place in a downtown Tokyo restaurant trying to appear confident in the fine art of Asian dining. Our group cozies up on stools at a u-shape counter to watch our cook set the preparations in motion for each of us to cook Shabushabu. It is a Japanese hotpot dish of thinly sliced meat and vegetables boiled in water. The term is an onomatopoeic one, derived from the sound emitted when the ingredients are stirred in the cooking pot and served with dipping sauces.

Our tour guide explains the procedure to us while we are coming to the restaurant. However, it all transpires faster in front of me. The counter is a madhouse of downtown lunch diners on a break from work. I put my vegetables—Chinese cabbage, carrots, onions and shitake mushrooms—in the pot, and stir them while the pot's broth made from kelp heats up.

I am supposed to submerge a slice of beef with my chopsticks, hold it in the soup and bring it out and dip it into sesame seed sauce first. It sounds easy until half my raw meat floats in the pot cooking to a well-done state, and I find no polite way to retrieve the strips with my inadequate chopstick skill. The young sales clerks across from me get a good look at my disaster, and I am sure they will have a decent amount of pantomime role-playing to do when they return to the shop. It is hit and miss whether or not I get out many vegetables. Out of necessity, I inhale most of the white steamed rice in the bowl. Supposedly, once the meat and vegetables have been eaten, leftover broth from the pot is customarily combined with the remaining rice, and the resulting soup is usually eaten last. The chef does that for me, and my broth is filled with bits of meat and vegetables. He offers me a spoon, and I am no longer ashamed of my manners. I'll chalk this one up to a bad chopstick day.

About halfway through the second week, it is inevitable that my friend and I both get a hankering for a good old-fashioned pizza, and when we see an Italian place, we look at each other with grins on our faces and decide to do it. It is another small restaurant in a mall, and this time the waitress speaks fairly good English, and she is well trained as a server. I want a glass of wine and explain to her that I favor a dry red, she nods and the next thing you know, she returns to the table with two small samples for me to try. Nice touch on her part, and I appreciate her extra effort. Our pizza is a thin crust Brooklyn style, and it is worth every mouthful. The craving for American food is over, and never again do I go searching. I am hardly ever homesick for meals at home, except occasionally for my cereal, fruit and yogurt breakfast routine. I attribute that to eating larger meals the first thing in the morning to fortify myself for the day's tour, or at least that's my rationale for taking a second helping of salmon salad on the buffet.

The majority of our meals are Japanese; however, a couple times our tour guide takes us to French restaurants in cities for lunches to mix it up a bit. The meals are excellent all the way from the tender coq au vin to the creamy pastries. In comparison, Japanese desserts are small scoops of ice cream and sometimes a green tea flavored cookie.

The final night before my departure we go as a group by private taxis to a restaurant in a neighborhood on a cul-de-sac with a very small sign outside. You would never notice it, nor have any reason to drive on this street unless you knew your destination. Evidently this out of the way place is one that the Japanese Prime Minister brings important dignitaries to for meals in one of the private dining rooms. Could John Kerry, our State Department Secretary have been here recently? I would love to think of the important business conducted informally at the very table where I am to be seated.

I am guided through a maze of halls leaving my shoes behind at the entrance, and like an important delegation, the design of the place made it so you never see another group anywhere. I come to our banquet room, seat myself at a low table and prepare to receive a delicious meal chosen by the chef themed around tofu. I have never seen tofu artfully dished in all sorts of combinations, almost like floral arranging on a dish. Each course is delightful and the plum wine complements it well.

Not all members of our group are tofu fans, and I think most of them are distracted packing their suitcases in their minds for the trip home. The splendor is slightly lost with the low comments, and I ignore them eating my last meal in peace. After the meal I return back down the hill to the hotel. I know that tomorrow brings airplane food, and my Asian dining is over.

I ate in tiny street restaurants elbow-to-elbow, fancy private dining rooms, on a second floor overlooking a river and in a rural village far away from the havoc of the city. I have my fondest ones, and the meals that will stay with me in my mind. Often I will be able to recollect a certain day from visualizing what I ate in the restaurant by taking pictures with my cell phone as tacky as it is and so overworked. At least I don't walk around with a selfie stick like so many other tourists from other countries. Pictures help. People at home are curious about foods from other countries, and I have examples.

The interactions with my dinner mates are most valuable, and those conversations will be cherished. We come from all parts of the United States and our lives are very different in many ways, yet each has a lot to contribute. We talk about our interests, other trips we have taken and our aspirations for future travel. After all, that's where I got the idea to come to Japan in the first place. I was sitting at a good-bye dinner in Barcelona last year. One of our group members from Toronto had done this very trip as a single traveler and encouraged me to give it a go. Sometimes you just need that extra prodding, and looking back a year ago, I made the right decision.

The Apex of Mindfulness

The humidity is high. The ground is slippery with a coating of moss from not getting the proper hours of sunlight. The steps—what ones remain—are crooked, steep and lack handrails. Those are the conditions I face the first thing in the morning on a tour to reach Senkoji Temple, a 400-year old temple nestled in the hillside above Kyoto.

The temple is partially funded for restoration by the Grand Circle Foundation, the parent tour company I use for travel. Once a prayer temple for Emperor Gosaga, it was severely damaged by a major typhoon back in 1959. It has been a struggle financially to rebuild the main hall as the number of visitors has significantly declined. Philanthropy and charity are not common in Japan, and many temples run side businesses to raise funds and act more like commercial organizations than religious ones. The temple handrails and step restoration on the main approach slope is a work in progress. Eventually, the whole path will be completed.

First I have to get there. Carrying my umbrella—the forecast is ominous —in case of a downpour, it comes in handy as a walking stick while I wind the forest-lined path. I can't help but perspire from the hot thick air and it doesn't help in breathing easily either. I'll admit being a little nervous and my heart is fluttering faster than a baby bird. The words I read in the travel materials before I left suggest this trip for "fit and active adults." Am I kidding myself?

There are twelve of us walking at different rates up to meet a Zen Buddhist priest who will do meditation and perform a tea ceremony—a ritual that repeated several times while I am in Japan. Amidst a little grumbling and complaining, a few of my fellow travelers don't want to put forth the effort, and they never get the full value in this particular discovery in my opinion. I decide not to engage in any further conversation as I have my own thoughts lingering, and I don't want them tainted by negativity.

In this case, I want purity and enlightenment from within myself. Each of us feels differently about a similar moment, and that's what makes the world go around and around. When you let the influence of other people sway you, you are not staying true to yourself. Maturity has enabled me to emphatically hold to my own feelings and viewpoints and absorb all that I am able. The mountaintop trip is a unique travel opportunity that all the books or videos in the world couldn't capture completely for me. You have to be there.

My mindset is different, though, and I recognized a change come over me after a few minutes of struggling. With each step I am conquering another obstacle, and I am reaching out higher and higher testing myself against nature. A slight slip or two on a crooked stone, and I am reminded that nothing worthwhile is easy in life ever. Oh, I've fallen and dropped off the path before me when I should have known better in my youthful days. Certain events put me in awe that I even knew to do the right thing when I look back over life. Lots of times there were other special people along the way to guide me, and other times, I had to do it on my own. The path is not straight, nor simple. It is tangled with obstacles and detours.

Perhaps, this whole trip is challenging my stamina and inner strength in a new way. You want to think that with age you are still capable of feats of physical strength, and on the flipside, you have the common sense to know when to back off. I am doing just fine. When I return to the hotel I believe I allow myself a few moments to relish in my accomplishment—it is good to mark special feats—and stay with the moment before thinking of something else, or what's next.

Holding on to a special moment is priceless. I think that it does wonders for your mental health, for too often you rush through things without taking in the complete experience. At home I keep a monthly journal of the highlights—events I attended, accomplishments, people connections—and before the first of the next month, I reread all those entries and spend a few moments reliving those heady feelings. How quickly I forget a meeting with friends for lunch, or a surprise that came in the mail.

My daily habit when I wake up in the morning before starting writing for a couple hours is a quiet meditation and prayer period in my special seat—a vintage orange upholstered chair in my living room. I free my mind of all thoughts and plans for the day, let my cat hop on my lap and listen to his breathing, which incidentally, reminds me to slow my own down. Breathing in and out over and over, my head lifts higher, my shoulders drop and I feel my jaw relaxing. No matter with what problem I am struggling—the loss of a dear friend, or the confusion over what project to tackle first—it gets answered thoughtfully. The reply might not be exactly what I am looking for, or there could be dead silence—I consider that an answer, too, for the time being. My time schedule from my small place in the universe and God's don't necessarily go together. I wait. Patiently. There comes a day when...

It is a pilgrimage of sorts for me slowly ascending in preparation for meeting with the priest. The gentle miniature waterfalls rushing down from the mountainside are the only sounds of nature and it is meant to be restful. I start turning inward and letting my heart open to my immediate surroundings. Once in awhile through the dense shrubs I get a glimpse of Kyoto off in the distance and the thick clouds that could bring a thunderstorm. The sky is both turbulent in its rolling movement and exotic in its streaks of deep tones of gray. How will I ever make it down safely? It is wise to drop that thought, for it is a fear that I don't want to get in the way.

Somewhere closer to my destination, I hear the first people in our group talking and when I round a bend, there is the priest waiting for us with his dog in tow. He'll lead us the rest of the way offering bamboo poles to help now that there is nothing to hang onto. I take a pole while the priest bows. Occasionally I use both my umbrella and the pole to propel me forward. The diminutive priest, not more than five-feet tall, wears a simple tan robe covering his body with his bare feet sticking out. His bald head framed an almost half smile face. As he turns forward on the path, he gives a nod for us to follow. I watch his sure-footedness tackle the path with the confidence of one who comes back and forth every day, which he does, to the town where he lives with his family.

There is no right word—"joyous," perhaps—to describe the moment that I make it to the temple, a simple Japanese style building with wide windows and tan tatami floor mats. The priest rests on his knees near the altar with one hand propped on his chin and looks at us in silence. He is setting the tone for sacredness to seep into our skin. The rest of us need to calm down and let the world's problems and what to do in our free time go in the afternoon. There isn't a sound except for a hawk's cry swooping on an air current out beyond the temple disturbing my concentration. I stare out at the woods around me mostly into the charcoal sky and am grateful for getting this far; honestly, I am hot and a little uncomfortable from sweat dripping down my backside. My breathing slows and I wedge into the tan cushion on the ledge. I am getting ready. I want to physically, mentally and spiritually be in harmony with nature.

After a few minutes the priest offers us a wafer—a sweet snack—and I nibble at it slowly. That's another thing: the pace and slowing down is necessary to get anything out of the experience, or any one. I come from a hurry up society, and often I forget the reason for eating, for nutrition and sustenance, should be honored. When you eat quickly, it is not good for your digestion, and you often eat a larger quantity, too. I will confess that my excuse for slowing down my eating in Japan is using chopsticks, which I handle relatively well after a lot of extra practice sessions thanks to YouTube during the winter.

Each of us has a small bowl filled with powdered matcha tea and a bamboo whisk on the low table set out in front of us. The priest comes around with boiling water in a large iron teapot that appears to have seen many years of service and pours some in each bowl. I am told to pick up the whisk and beat the mixture back and forth until the tea foams slightly. The priest inspects each bowl. When he comes to me, he takes the whisk from me and stirs more vigorously, and nods that it is ready to drink. The taste is somewhat bitter, but all sorts of energy comes welling up from my insides. It could be from the snack, too. I am revived and ready to listen to his talk on Zen Buddhism.

Zen is a branch of Buddhism thought that believes divine wisdom resides in each person and through specific meditation techniques this nature is revealed. The priest rang a bell and tells us to be still into ourselves for five minutes and let our minds clear of mundane things. I do. It is wonderful and satisfying at the same time.

Throughout the years I have taken yoga and studied comparative religions; I have a good idea of what the priest would tell us. He patiently answers questions, too, and explains how one closes his heart to the world's desires. That is a hard concept for some to grasp in our group. The priest says that you are constantly bombarded unless you pull away and free your emotions from such control. It is a continual struggle within you. The aim is rid oneself of attachments on this earth for they are only temporary.

This session is one I am living out, and I rejoice in my own personal way with my God right there, everywhere all the time. My walk down the hill will be no problem at all. The rain holds off and on the last step before touching the level path, I thank God for such a special experience. So far away from home, and here I am having a worshipful moment that I will cherish always. It' s certainly a mountaintop ah ha.

Temple Charm

A friend hands me a large brown manila folder filled with information about temples, shrines and gardens a couple months before I travel, and when I pulled out her material, not a single photo prepares me for what I witness in Japan. Vibrant colors. Gold leaf scrolled designs on pillars. Massive structures. I am overwhelmed.

There is no planned order to my discussions about particular shrines and temples, and I only share a little of what stands out. That's enough to give you the idea. Now that I am looking back, I am reliving those visits in my mind without the interference of throngs of people, high humidity and pesky raindrops. My friend's booklets are helping, too, for fully appreciating those encounters.

I find that Buddhism and Shinto are complex religions, and I am only scratching the surface with a long way to go for deeper understanding. As a Christian, I face the same problem walking my faith daily. There is always more, and I dig deeper within myself to find meaning. Often, I must just trust and allow things to unfold. It never fails, though, that a wise person comes my way and steers me in a direction that surprises even myself. I move ahead for a time and am grateful.

A Buddhist refers to a temple as his holy place, and a shrine is the term in the Shinto religion. Since Sunday is not marked on the calendar as a regular day to worship like in Christianity or Judaism, believers flock to temples and shrines on special celebrations or on random days when they have the time to honor the gods.

People typically rinse their hands and mouth with water in a basin or pool located at the entrance to a temple gate. It's a purification process. A temple had a set of ladles, and the final step is to hold one up like a mirror to see into your heart's reflection. A father picks his two preschoolers one by one and shows both what he was doing. They laugh together.

Occasionally I am taking photos at an outside altar while a couple next to me is making an offering to the gods with their hands put together, chanting a few words while clearing their minds and bowing. I try to be respectful. First, they clap their hands together and ring bells to attract the shrine's spirits to come and hear their prayers.

A priest is often giving a private service—people pay to have him perform it—within an enclosed area closer to the Buddha. I watch from a distance, and I politely back away. I don't want to be a disturbance with my curiosity, and I honor others who have concerns that require prayer and attention.

As a country the Japanese are 60 percent Buddhist, 60 percent Shinto and 60 percent atheists. Those figures don't add up. It's meant for emphasis.

So, where does superstition play into it?

Good luck charms are Japanese amulets (charms, talismans) commonly sold at religious sites and dedicated to particular Shinto deities and Buddhist figures and are said to provide various forms of luck or protection. Originally made from paper or wood, modern amulets are small items usually kept inside a brocade bag and may contain a prayer, religious inscription of invocation They are available at both Shinto shrines and Buddhist temples with few exceptions and are available for sale, regardless of one's religious affiliation.

Omamori are then made sacred through the use of ritual, and are said to contain busshin: spiritual offshoots, in a Shinto context or kesshin, a manifestations in a Buddhist context. While omamori are intended for temple tourists' personal use, they are mainly viewed as a donation to the temple or shrine the person is visiting. Visitors often give omamori as a gift to another person as a physical form of well-wishing. Japanese have probably always believed in amulets of one type or another, but the modern printed charms now given out by shrines and temples first became popular in the Tokugawa period (1600-1800), and the practice of wearing miniature charms on one's person is also new. The latter custom is particularly common in cities, and I noticed women wearing them around their necks. Now I understand its significance.

Japan has a turbulent history of devastating wars, earthquakes, fires, tsunami, typhoons, crop failures, epidemics and volcanic eruptions. It's little wonder that numerous ways to obtain good luck are valued as traditions or culture even amongst those who don't believe in luck.

Omikuji are paper fortunes that are sold at temples and shrines in Japan. Approximately half of Omikuji predict some level of bad luck. When this happens, it's customary to leave the fortune behind by tying it at a designated spot. I spotted tons of trees and fences covered with those bad luck papers. A good fortune is kept for a few months until the person feels the luck has run out. Several people in my group purchase them, and there are mixed reactions over what they read. I know that I will not attempt to interfere with my own fate.

Putting seriousness aside, I come across two young Japanese women hovering over one fortune paper at a pool of flowing water. Something tells me that I might have a couple amusing pictures. I ask to photograph the scene not knowing the outcome. The writing is in indelible ink. One of them dips it in and the "magic writing" starts to show up. The look on her face is priceless. She blushes and the two girls break up laughing. Something awesome is about to happen to her I am sure—a new boyfriend, an engagement. I only wish the best for her.

Ema are wooden prayer boards available for purchase at Japanese shrines. A person purchases a board, writes his prayers and wishes on the back and leaves it hanging at the shrine. Ema stack up quickly. They are regularly collected and burned by the shrine.

In most cases—there is one exception at Senkoji Temple on a private tour—I am viewing a magnificent site in crowded conditions with a combination of stepping around gawking tourists and those Japanese people on a spiritual mission. It doesn't leave me much room for developing any personal insights, or feeling very deeply. Besides, on a couple days the rain comes down in buckets and I stay under an umbrella only lifting it a second or two to get a full perspective of a giant structure.

One morning the first stop is in Nara at Todaiji Temple, and my greeters are free-roaming deer, sacred creatures that roam about on the grounds. They attract a lot of attention and are quite tame. School children feed two or three at a time, and they have a hard time getting away from their "new friends." Those deer are persistent. At another temple in a different setting the sacred deer choose to pick at my clothes and sniff at what I have to offer. I am warned, and I don't take it seriously. Sure enough, one pokes at my blue bag I thought I had hidden behind my back, and takes off with it. Fortunately a couple little children near me run after the deer and pull my package out of his mouth. The girls bow to me, and I bow back thanking them for helping me retrieve my package.

I've seen too many deer in the wild to be amused by these herds, scrawny and with patches of fur missing. I am more interested in the buildings, though. Dailbutsu-den Hal is the largest wooden building in the world and the home of Nara' Great Buddha—a massive 52-foot statue of the Vairocana Budda made from cast bronze. The off white and black-trimmed edifice stands proudly, and I will be taken back at what I see inside. An impressive site is the 1001 standing statutes of the Buddhist deity—simply called Kannon, the Buddhist goddess of mercy—at the Sanjusangen-do Temple. They are lined up in rows like soldiers across the massive hall, and it is hard to take my eyes of them. I am transfixed. Since photos are not allowed, I buy a gold-leaf file folder just for the picture.

The region is known for the craft of gold leaf. These thin sheets of gold have been produced in Kanazawa since the 16th century, and are used to decorate handicrafts to Buddhist altars. Beating gold into an extremely thin sheet with a thickness of 0.1 to 0.125 makes a gold leaf. It is so thin that if you rub it with your hands, it will come off.

Later I go to Kasuga Shinto Shrine admiring its many sub-shrines—it gets confusing—and stroll along a wooded path up and down stairs with its collection of three thousand stone lanterns. Some are draped in moss, and others have patches of flowers surrounding them.

Very impressive is the Fushimi-Inari Shrine, dedicated to the gods of rice and sake, and today is know for its hundreds of torii gates, which cover the trails. Approximately 10,000 torii gates stand on the grounds, thanks to the contributions of worshippers nationwide as a testament for their answered prayers. What strikes me is the rich vermillion color, which symbolizes the life force and counteracts spells.

When I get home I write:

Taking a risk means walking a path where you don't see the exact outcome. That's how you grow and become more confident. Be thankful for all those in your life who stood back after giving you guidance and let you find your own way.

That is exactly how my feet are walking me through a set of those gates up a hill that bends and changes direction with no indication as to how far, or where I will end up. It is rather exciting to experiment and let things fall into place without any control issues getting the better of me.

On a soaking rain sort of damp day, I visited The Golden Pavilion of the Rokuon-Ji Temple, and strolling the circular path, I pause for a photo across the pond with lovely beds of purple iris in the foreground. Somehow the rain doesn't quite make the gold leaf on the temple's outer covering sparkle, and it is a subdued experience shrouded in dark gray.

On the very last afternoon before returning home on Ikuchijima Island, I visit the dazzling Kosanji Temple, built by the Buddhist priest Kozo Kosanji to honor his mother and took more than thirty years to build. Actually, I am   hot and tired if I remember correctly, and our group is on a residential street, when out of nowhere come the steps to this temple. "Wow," is all I heard from around me. It is a final homage to the faith. I always have been an avid believer of making the most of little incidences that appear out of thin air and make life a little bit more fun. Those small impromptu moments can lift me up for days at a time and bring on a spirited mood.

On a high hill above the temple area is Miraishin no Oka—The Heights of Eternal Hope for the Future—a white marble sculpture garden created by world-renowned artist Katuzo Kuetani towers over the entire area. The sun's hot rays beating down on the purity of the stone inform that the world is far more massive than meets the eye. Visitors hop on and off the rocks for the perfect pose, and all in all, the majesty of the grounds rubs off. I listen for the whispered hymns of the ancients and the hourglass passage of time, while the miniature pebbles under my feet shuffle here and there.

The elevator takes me down to reality again, and I hurry back to the dock to leave on the hydrofoil for the mainland. By the time I am back in Hirsoshima, I am cooled off and glad that I didn't carry an unnecessary jacket or sweater with me. I did bring a slice of octopus freeze-dried in a thin plastic wrapper. "You are taking home...what?" That will go on the grill lightly broiled later this summer as a reminder of my last full day in Japan. The god of cooking is blessing my purchase.

Tradition Tradition

Photographs are expressions of how people find meaning in daily life. I move quickly and take as many snaps one right after the other in hopes that one will be *the* shot. I capture the serene face of a geisha close-up bordered by a silk curtain, and it leaps off the print. I ask her questions—her age when she started in training school, her apprenticeship and more importantly, why she chose that lifestyle. Two tiny schoolboys in blue uniforms holding hands are tagging a little behind their classmates. They both have an impish expression not so different than boys anywhere else in the world. They wave at me with the peace sign and run on happily.

Then again, certain scenes come across well for there is a story to tell beyond what one initially is framed in the lens. Take the picture I snapped at the Tokyo hotel in an alcove on my floor. In the vending machine you can buy water, soda, iced tea and two kinds of beer. That simple wow moment intrigues me—so different than all the legalities at home. Or the picture of washi, a thick fibrous paper made from mulberry bark, I took in a rural community for years isolated from city life. Craftspeople continue to make handmade journals, lampshades and wall hangings from paper they have crafted. Both are commentaries on how modern life and the past intersect.

After clicking animated close-up pictures of a dozen young couples dressed in kimonos and sandals with their hair styled in uplifts strolling around a garden near a temple, my tour guide quietly whispers to me that they are Japanese tourists themselves who have rented costumes for a couple hours just to have a little pleasure on an outing. It's not the real deal. I start to notice more carefully and become more discriminating pulling out my camera.

When a parade of Chinese get off their tour bus as a group dressed in costume, I no longer rush for the camera. The best photo op on a late afternoon, though, is mingling with a group of University of Michigan students dressed authentically while visiting a Shinto shrine having a grand time parading around in their finery shouting, "Go Wolverines." It reminds me of how people often partake in a Renaissance Faire where they live the period getting pleasure out of it as participants. How often I run into a former student or two at the Sterling Renaissance Faire in Upstate New York near Fair Haven that loved the period when they first learned about it in school, and continue on engaged with it after meeting Will Shakespeare's fine work in high school and college.

Like in every other country in the world, springtime is perfect for weddings, and what better place to be in Japan for the photography session, than in a garden blooming with azalea bushes nears a shrine or temple. The bride and groom are decked out in traditional kimonos. The first such couple—the bride dressed in a flowing white robe and the groom in a black one holding a parasol over them—poses and is arranged by the photographer's assistant on a small bridge overlooking a bank of purple iris. They beam when the rest of us hold out our cell phones and cameras, too, like they are celebrities. Well, they are for an important day in their lives together as husband and wife. After seeing several more couples in other gardens during my stay, the last pair turns out to be tourists from Taiwan outfitted in wedding regalia just for fun letting us all take their pictures among the tall bamboo forest garden. What can I say? I bought in like the rest of the crowd and no harm done.

At home I have seen Japanese tourists at the local rest stop taking pictures of things that seem all too common to me—the gas pumps, the bicycle chained outside to a pole and the overflowing trash basket—and I take a double look at what it might be that intrigues them. I understand all three items better after my visit. The Japanese have many hybrid cars in cities, and they have recharging stations in parking lots and at gas stations. Might they wonder why we are still using fossil fuel? Bicycles are left all day unlocked in tiered garages in cities. As for the trash receptacles, they are not common items found in public places.

Once my husband and I were at a park camped in our motor home overnight. The windows were closed and the large curtain covered the front window. Upon waking in the morning after a sound sleep, I thought I heard a twitter or two, and I went to the driver's seat and parted the curtain just a tiny bit to see what might be happening. Here was a busload of Japanese tourists lined up for a group photo in front of our camper. I'm glad that we were able to oblige. How they must have marveled at the bigness of everything from people to recreational vehicles.

It isn't a planned stop in Tokyo; however, after a discussion with our tour leader about the work ethic of mid level employees in Tokyo, she takes us to explore The Capsule Hotel, an example of accommodations where employers put up workers if they require them to be on the job beyond the normal 12 hour days. It is cheaper for the employer rather than paying to send a worker home for just a few hours of sleep. After taking off my shoes and using the elevator in the lobby of a sparsely decorated building, I come to a plain hall and walk past rows and rows of stacked cubicles in twos each large enough to sleep a normal size man. A TV monitor and a temperature control switch is all that is in each cubicle, along with a pull down shade for privacy. Showering and dressing are done down the hall in a group room. My first reaction after watching one of the larger men in our tour group try to fit into a cubicle, is that my cat has larger boarding kennel space. When I told that to my tour guide, she gasped in disbelief.

While visiting with three housewives in the city of Kameoka not far from Kyoto, and engaging in a conversation about their lives, I find out that each of their husbands works long hours and makes decent salaries. The women stay at home running the household and the children basically see their fathers on weekends, and often only one of those days, too, as fathers may be working. None of the women have careers, and from what I could gather, that is pretty standard in Japan. There are 5 paid sick days and 10 vacation days in their husbands' job agreement, yet employees are discouraged from using them. Interestingly enough, these women have a little part time venture as their children are teenagers and are in school. They invite traveling guests to a Heiki residence dating back eight generations to the founder, a magistrate in the shogun family-style government to learn the art of making ball sushi and serve a lunch.

The Heiki residence's front gate, stones, mud walls and ceilings are carefully maintained as it was built in the late Tokugawa period with its capital in Edo, which today is modern Tokyo. I see the actual palanquin, which was used by the first Master Heiki. In the main guest room there are sliding doors and partitions with crane paintings, vintage bows and arrows and archery equipment. I walk through several rooms before arriving at the dining area.

The women are proficient teachers and first show how they prepare the vinegary rice by slicing through it many times to keep the texture sticky. I make four balls of rice. I am given a plate of cooked salmon, omelet, fresh cucumber and steamed shrimp to lay over the top of each ball before decorating with thin slices of Japanese honewort—from the parsley family —wasabi, tomato and pickle. It is finger licking yummy and making me hungry for the housewives meal, which is soon placed in front of me.

It is a pleasure to view the photo albums that the housewives pass around the table, and I admire every one. Each tells us about her children's interests and hobbies outside of school. Saturdays and Sundays students take classes in the arts and sports since the regular school week is devoted to academic studies. As children get into the middle grades, they attend cram school from 4-7 pm evenings. In fact, there is a cram school next door to my hotel later on in Hiroshima, and I see children dutifully coming to classes. In order for their high schoolers to get into college, the housewives say that they have a rigorous homework schedule, too, after cram school allowing only four hours of sleep per night if they want to be accepted into the best colleges. It is a way of life, and Japanese school years are to be taken seriously from what I am hearing from the housewives. Education is a high priority.

One evening I am invited to the home of two professional musicians well known for their performance and teaching ability with ancient instruments of Japan. They lead me up a flight of stairs in my stocking feet and I am seated on the floor for a private concert. The lady plays a long slender three-stringed instrument, a shamisen, dating back to the 16 century and the gentleman performs with a bamboo flute. It is called a shakuhachi, a Japanese end-blown flute, which was originally introduced from China into Japan. Accomplished players can produce virtually any pitch they wish from the instrument, and play a wide variety of songs. This is made easier by the wicker baskets that the monks wore over their heads, a symbol of their detachment from the world. The gentleman uses a wicker basket in his demonstration so that I will better understand.

Music is quite a lovely respite and speaks a universal language all over the world. Whether it is in the studio of Japanese musicians, at a campfire in the Texas foothills or the folkloric tango dancing on the stage Buenos Aires, a bond is fostered among people.

After leaving I go by taxi to the heart of Koyoto's Gion Corner where I walk the cobblestone street and take in the charm of old Koyoto with its wooden buildings and old-style inns before settling in to a restaurant. I spot a black chauffeured limo driving through the crowded street with a geisha sitting erectly in the passenger's seat looking straight a head. My camera doesn't come out in time.

On my final afternoon in Koyoto I attend a special theatre performance, the 179th Kamogawa Odori, a dance and drama spectacle by the geisha of the city. Ponto-cho is a small district along a narrow street and is the home of the geisha, who have long continued to devote themselves to the arts. The annual event in May showcases splendid sets and traditional Japanese dancing. A formal tea ceremony opens the event and a geisha is outfitted in a gorgeous formal kimono with her obi tied in the back. Her style of wig depicts the difference between a maiko, an apprentice, and her. Her face is in white make-up and is certainly remarkable—you turn your head for a second look while she goes through the ritual almost like a marionette, with her movements in utter silence oblivious to her audience.

Earlier in the trip I went to a teahouse in Kawazawa city and found out about the role of the geisha in performing for businessmen with conversation and music to this day, not any different than in years past. Often misconstrued as more than what meets the eye, and on the sleazy side, too, that is not the case for the geisha in Japanese society.

Surrounding almost every hotel in the bigger cities is a pachinko parlor, and it is a popular game that originated in Japan. Basically, it is a mechanical slot machine with characters you want to line up in threes for the jackpot. It fills a gambling niche comparable to that of the slot machine in Western gaming. I don't go in to the one on the block near my hotel. There is no English spoken, and honestly, I am not much of a gambler to begin with anyhow.

I observe several ceremonial tea ceremonies or chanoyu, and each experience is a slowing down process of myself as well as for the proper way with tea. Each time I am able to slip away a tiny bit longer and appreciate the idleness of my body and mind. Tea is my drink of choice and the fresh leaves brewing in teapots become much more meaningful to me each day.

A lot of activities in Japan have remained for centuries, and there is an appreciation for them by the people of the country.

Zodiac Signs, Language and Museums

"Cheerful, popular and quick witted. Self-reliant and impetuous. A showy dresser. Loves to exercise both mentally and physically. As skillful in business as in love."

Yup. All of the above. That's my Asian zodiac chart reading lining up with my birth year.

My tour guide hands our group the chart. She won't tell us her age outright, and instead, suggests that we identify her key characteristics, and go from there. Throughout our days together, she gives out other clues off-handedly about the popular music and dress style she embraces as a teen. It puts her growing up in the early 80s. She dances around giving a straight answer at the farewell banquet. (I think she is 50.) I hear before I come to Japan that a Japanese person doesn't outwardly use the word, "no." If that had anything to do with her evasive answer, I am not aware.

As for my birth year, I am going to let you guess—if it matters at all. Women in Japan age gracefully and have a chic style whenever they are out in public. Four ladies chatting over tea together in a restaurant in Kyoto are groomed immaculately and have their nails in various shades of red. It's hard to figure out if they are near my age or not. The fact that they are enjoying each other's company is what is more important.

The Chinese Zodiac, known as Sheng Xiao, is based on a twelve-year cycle, each year in that cycle related to an animal sign. These signs are the rat, ox, tiger, rabbit, dragon, snake, horse, sheep, monkey, rooster, dog and pig. It is calculated according to the Chinese lunar calendar and very popular in Asian countries such as Japan.

Although it sounds a bit superstitious, Japanese people take their year of birth seriously. According to soothsaying, people in their own Ben Ming Nian, the Zodiac sign for their birth year, may offend "Taisui," also called the God of Age, causing them to suffer a lot of misfortunes, such as sickness, economic loss, physical injuries and obstacles in careers. However, there are effective ways to diminish the unlucky impacts. The most popular solution is wearing red underwear, socks or waist belts given by elders, for red is believed to bring them good luck. Some jewelry accessories may also help, such as pendants and bracelets with auspicious images.

I am not sure what the fascination is for Japanese women and logo apparel until my tour guide says that it is all about following trends feverishly because the population is so superstitious by nature. One evening I watch twenty and thirty year olds—even women much older—in a Koyto department store intently looking over expensive Hello Kitty bracelets and pendants, and I am mistaken that the Japanese bobtail cat with the red bow is no longer in vogue. Its popularity hasn't waned.

Back in the 70s, Hello Kitty, a fictional character produced in Japan by Sanrio, was created by Yuko Shimizu but is currently designed by Yuko Yamaguchi. Shortly after her creation in 1974, Hello Kitty greeted the world with a "Hello!" on her first product. Sanrio introduced the iconic Hello Kitty vinyl coin purse in March 1975. The character was then brought to the United States in 1976. Originally marketed to pre-adolescent females, Hello Kitty's target has broadened to include adult consumers. She can be found on a variety of products ranging from school supplies to fashion accessories, high-end consumer products and including various diamond necklaces. Several Hello Kitty TV series written for elementary school age children have been produced, and Hello Kitty is also the main character at the two Japanese Sanrio theme parks.

As for the Japanese language, it is highly contextualized and situational depending if it is a formal or casual conversation. The age of people talking together and their social status is taken into account, too.

I barely master the very basic words and phrases: yes – hai; please for a request – onegai shimasu; thank you – arigatoo gozaimu su; good bye – sayonara; good morning – ohayo gozaimasu. I am able to greet the chambermaid—or man—cleaning my room and thank a shopkeeper at the mall.

Most of the time restaurant wait staff and store clerks speak enough English to get by, and with pictures on the menu in certain places, I make it. One evening my friend and I are dining in a restaurant, and the waitress immediately brings over a Frenchman who speaks English even before we open the menu. He is helpful, steers us in the right direction based on our eating likes and offers suggestions about what specials are on the menu. He comes out front between courses to continue on about why he moved to Japan to raise his children with his Japanese wife. He connects to the culture he readily answers. In the meantime, it turns out he is the head chef and races back to prepare our food. There's nothing like having personal attention, and the chef's French-Asian fusion style is admirable.

Other times with older people having less frequent opportunities to speak English, such as museum directors and artisans, they work through an interpreter to get their specialized messages across. I am thinking about a craftsman in Hakone who designed wooden inlaid products, or mosaic woodwork based on the techniques of an ancient craftsman toward the end of the Edo era. The mountains around Hakone are blessed with natural colors and shades of wood and the craftsman takes advantage to form geometric patterns. Today the craftsman uses a technique with a jig saw to slice into thin sheets with a special plane to allow mass production.

My favorite piece in the shop is a secret box, which seems to have no opening, and you can't tell which side is the top or bottom. To open the box you have to push and pull at the sides in a correct order. It reminds me of a rubric cube and how patience pays off if you are willing to commit the time to work it through. There's that element of quietness, too, in your mind free of other distractions allowing the juices to flow.

The Japanese borrow the Chinese script system, and it simply looks artistic. Each kanji, or Chinese character, has a meaning. For example, the character for god can be read jin, and the one for house ja. A jinja, or shrine, is a place where the god lives. A local shrine holds a deep meaning for communities in Japan.

What makes the Japanese written system so complicated is that there are two other types of characters—hiragana and katakana as well as kanji. Hiragana and katakana are simpler characters that represent sounds only. Confused? I am, and marvel that Japanese children learn about 80 kanji—there are 2000—characters and hiragana and katakana in their first year of elementary school.

Nichi means sun and hon means the place where something begins. In ancient times when emissaries and merchants from Japan traveled to China, they are said to have referred to the land east of China as the land of the rising sun: Nippon or Nihon. I fly to Japan on Nippon Airlines across the International Dateline into the eastern sky.

I never fail to visit museums and art galleries any place where I am traveling, and Japan is no exception. When my tour guide tells me this particular museum we would be stopping to tour became one of Japan's most controversial sites in 1979 when fourteen class-A war criminals were enshrined there, I not sure what to expect. Outside of Tokyo is the Yasukuni Shrine, a memorial completed in 1869 to honor the 2.5 million people who have died in war. While its name means, "Peace of the Country," it is a military museum in all respects. In the open entry is a Mitsubishi carrier-type fighter plane from World War II, and the story of Japanese in war begins from displays of early samurai swords dedicated to the deity not only as weapons but also as symbols of the spirits, to the modern one-man sub used to sink ships.

This is my first encounter with understanding the Japanese mindset about war and destruction, and my tour guide handles it bravely and tactfully by always pulling the comments back to the importance of Japan seeking and maintaining a national peace. The artifacts from soldiers in many wars who sacrificed their lives for love of their country are displayed in their honor.

Before I leave I hold back a little from the others. I want to be alone for a few minutes in quiet and reverence. I pass by wall after wall of pictures with names and dates of service and thought of the similar sad feelings I have visiting the Viet Nam Memorial in Washington D.C. These are faces of young boys barely teens and older decorated soldiers who believed in their country. Looking at major world events through the eyes of people from a different perspective is a way to keep myself diverse.

I wander through large indoor markets in each city, and they are like living museums of the food culture. In Kanazawa the market has stalls filled with carnations, also, a national flower for Mother's Day and I watch last minute shoppers on a Saturday afternoon grabbing bouquets along with unfamiliar root vegetables and cooking herbs. Meat, poultry and fish have sections and I stop for a second or two to watch a vendor reach into an iced pile with his bare hands, pick out a handful of squid for a customer, weigh and wrap it in brown paper. Sale.

The Tokyo National Museum is a little intimidating with its floors of collections. Fortunately, my tour guide takes our group on a walk of the highlights and explains particular pieces in the roughly two hours we spend there. I am most amazed with the period costuming, decorative folding room screens and the ceramics. Calligraphy is another art form that is charming and it still flourishing today.

I love how those of other cultures visit their museums regularly as I see from the many Japanese families of all ages coming and going through the rooms together. One little girl around six gets ahead of her parents and deposits herself in the next room kicking her feet against the velvet couch. She is quickly brought back into line by a guard with a gentle tap of his hand on her legs. Her parents catch up with her. The next time I see her, she is one room ahead of her family again. That would be me at her age, and I sympathize with her plight tagging along with her parents when the world is opening before her.

In our country, I believe that we have lost the value of going to art galleries, museums and classical concerts. We are not appreciating and learning from our past. Silent walls are waiting to speak out and teach us lessons from the magnificent artifacts in national history museums and symphonic music composed by talented musicians, to the paintings of famous masters. Our museums are virtually empty except for tourists. Well, I may be exaggerating a bit to make my point. I applaud the Europeans for Sundays are set aside for family outings to museums. And they have no trouble finding time for cheering on their favorite soccer teams either. We have way too much invested in self-serving endeavors and our immediate gratification.

Looking Beyond Hiroshima

When I am making up my mind whether or not to take the trip, stopping in Hiroshima calls out to me every time. I should go there. It will finalize a period of history. Thus, my trip extends several more days.

On the closing days of my vacation, I spend the remainder in the modern city of Hiroshima with its wide boulevards, bustling stores and sleek buildings. Everything is rebuilt with functionality in mind—earthquake proof, too, for there are at least three a day—and the majority of the people walking the streets are two or three generations removed from the destruction. It has been over 70 years since 80% of the city was destroyed. On August 6, 1945, during World War II (1939-45), an American B-29 bomber dropped the world's first deployed atomic bomb over the Japanese city of Hiroshima.

After leaving my bag off at the hotel, I go to the actual place where the A-bomb hit. I anticipate that it will be a long afternoon, and I need plenty of time to process everything. That's the way my writing mind works in order to capture the spirit of somewhere.

There is a brief stop for a specialty lunch originating in Hiroshima. Okonomiyaki is classic Japanese street food that is often compared to Japanese pancakes. Okonomiyaki recipes can vary in ingredients. I watch the grill chef pour a thin batter the size of a medium plate, cover with cabbage, fish and assorted vegetables before flattening, pouring an egg over and browning on both sides. He pushes the finished dish to me off the grill with his large spatula. I slice it like a pizza with a smaller spatula, eat it with chopsticks and mostly with my fingers. It is a lot of food for lunch and I finish every morsel while the grill chef waits for my praise. It's a two thumbs–up meal.

As I stand in the park shaded by large trees looking at the one remaining building left as a symbol of the city's wipe-out and to the actual target—the bridge 200 feet away—tears well. Here I am halfway around the world to the faraway place that was the main topic so often in conversations during my childhood. Part of the panic about the Cold War period in the fifties was how horrible a nuclear war would be if the Russians used their weapon of destruction. The events at Hiroshima and Nagasaki were too close of a reminder. Those duck and cover drills at school scared me on Fridays, and it was the free ice cream in the cafeteria line that softened my anxieties somewhat. If we students behaved, we were handed our sweet treat by the ladies with a smile. I don't know what that had to do with the seriousness of impending doom.

Growing up, my history books are filled with how World War II ends abruptly and why bombing Japan is deemed necessary. It saves American soldiers lives and spares the Japanese people from more suffering. I don't debate the reason. Still, it is hard to fathom that at one moment in time there are human beings screaming in agony and racing to get away from the terrific heat—many jump into the river—and all the multitude of fires from collapsing buildings. Since it is so still around me—people are relatively into their own thoughts—a rush of energy circles me. It really is hard to describe, except I felt the identical energy at Gettysburg, Nuremberg and looking into the pit of earth at the 9/11 destruction before the museum was built. There's nothing like living the history of the world.

There are many Japanese middle school children here with their teachers studying the facts of the event, and I wonder what they are being told. Maybe it is me—a couple other Americans say they felt the same—but there is restlessness in the air when I come face-to-face with those children. In fact, a couple young girls somehow get mixed into our group, and when they look at us I hear one whisper to the other, "Oh, Americans." There is no negativity in her voice, except that they are studying about the country that dropped the A-bomb, and here we are in real time. From every other discussion I have in Japan, peace for the future is the most desired lesson to be taken away from a bad period.

Over at the Children's Peace Memorial there is a statue of Sadako, the girl who started making paper cranes in her hospital bed praying for her life, soon becomes her challenge for the children all over Japan. *Sadako and the 1000 Paper Cranes,* by Eleanoer Coerr, is a fictional retelling of the story of Sadako Sasaki who lived in Hiroshima at the time of the atomic bombing by the United States, Sadako is 2 years old when the atomic bomb is dropped near her home by Misasa Bridge. She is at home when the explosion occurred, about one mile from Ground Zero. In November 1954, when Sadako is 12 she develops swellings on her neck and behind her ears. In January 1955, purple spots form on her legs. Subsequently, she is diagnosed with leukemia her mother refers to it as "an atom bomb disease." She is hospitalized on February 21, 1955, and given, at the most, a year to live.

Sadako spends her time in a nursing home folding origami paper cranes in hopes of making a thousand of them. She is inspired to do so by the Japanese legend that one who created a thousand paper cranes has a wish come true. She wants to live. In this retelling of her story, Sadako manages to fold only 644 cranes before she becomes too weak to fold any more, and dies on the morning of 25 October 1955. Her friends and family help finish her dream by folding the rest of the cranes, which are buried with Sadako.

However, her surviving family members do not back up the claim in the book. According to her family, and especially her older brother Masahiro Sasaki, who speaks on his sister's life at events, Sadako not only exceeded 644 cranes, she exceeded her goal of 1000 and died having folded approximately 1,400 paper cranes. Mr. Sasaki and the family have donated some of Sadako's cranes at places of importance around the world: in NYC at the 9-11 memorial, and at Pearl Harbor, Hawaii. After her death, Sadako's friends and schoolmates publish a collection of letters in order to raise funds to build a memorial to her and all of the children who have died from the effects of the atomic bomb.

In 1958, a statute of Sadako holding a golden crane is unveiled in the Hiroshima Peace Memorial, also called the Genbaku Dome, and installed in the Hiroshima Peace Park. At the foot of the statue is a plaque that reads: "This is our cry. This is our prayer. Peace on Earth." Every year on Oban Day, which is a holiday in Japan to remember the departed spirits of one's ancestors, thousands of people leave paper cranes near the statue. They are symbols of eternal life and emissaries of death.

Sadako and the Thousand Paper Cranes was a favorite piece of literature in my elementary classroom for many years, and here I am standing in this special park fulfilling a promise I had made when I retired—tour the places in the world that I taught about from textbooks and videos.

A school is having a ceremony, children are reciting speeches and a couple representatives place a new colorful paper chain of cranes along with the others lining the monument. It is dignified and orderly, and I observed, the children in their navy uniforms are serious and focused.

An hour is spent with a survivor—a woman age six at the time—and she talks through a translator about what she remembers and hears from her family. I am not positive how much she actually witnessed herself and the clarity of her memory. She has given that same speech so many times that all her feelings are squeezed out of it, or perhaps, I am misinterpreting her intentions. It could be the way Japanese survivors relate to their past. In a soft, monotone voice she describes looking up at the bright cloud that rains ash down from the sky wondering what to make of it while she is on her school playground. She stays at the school building, partially damaged itself until evening, when the steam train is running again and she returns home. I've heard similar experiences from Holocaust survivors and with a lot more emotion. We tend to focus on the epic moments in history, and not the actual people who suffer sickness, death and hunger as a result. This lady is fortunate that she never has any lingering after affects from radiation like so many others. Looking into this survivor's face, I see a life well lived for a 76 year old woman, one who has come to a thoughtful conclusion about her childhood.

The Hiroshima Peace Memorial Museum collects the remains of the devastation and the horror of that event, and like walking through the 9/11 Memorial in NYC, there is hardly a sound among the crowd. In the brochure handed to me in English it states, "Hiroshima's deepest wish is the elimination of all nuclear weapons and the realization of a genuinely peaceful international community." I look. I take it in. It is not a place that I desire to return.

Not one to buy souvenirs much at gift shops, I find a three multi-colored paper crane Christmas ornament for the tree at home. My tour guide spells out to me that the Japanese like the tree idea, and have one on December 25 with presents and family gatherings. Buddhism and Shintoism are very tolerant of other religions, so Japanese people feel free to celebrate Christmas. They don't consider it a religious holiday. Christmas's modern origin is after WWII, when the Japanese mass media encourages people to buy electronics goods at Christmastime to help the economy.

All in all, I drop into bed exhausted. Never will I forget this sultry May day. It is a one-of-a kind.

On a lighter note, it is by staying in Hiroshima that I launch off by ferry to Miyajima for a day trip, an island that was once worshipped for its spirituality. I have no idea as to the intense beauty I was to uncover. I discern the grandeur of the Itsukushima Shinto Shrine, which is founded in AD 593, and consider it one of the finest examples of Japanese Shinden architecture.

The famed gate to the shrine, the otorii, rises from the blue seawater, its vermillion-colored pillars extending more than 40 feet above the seabed. The inner shrine includes 37 buildings, while the outer shrine near the shore consists of 19 structures all blending in with the natural beauty of the site. I snap so many pictures from every possible angle in the sparkling blue sky and attempt to take it all in. Magnificent. It is one of the times when I want to stick my two feet into the ground and never consider leaving.

When I return home and post a picture of the temple on Facebook, a friend, an expert timber frame builder, writes, "The temples of Japan are some of the most artful timber frames in existence and were built over generations. In many cases they cut the trees, then sank them in seawater for as long as 20 years as a means of preserving the wood. Hard to imagine a time before today's immediate gratification mindset. The Japanese craftsmen continue to set the standard of fine joinery."

That is the afternoon when I have Miyajima's specialty—oysters. I select a platter of grilled and fried—no raw choice—and the large plumb, tender oysters are delicious. Poking and prodding those slippery devils with chopsticks is another matter. The chardonnay pairing works well to keep my cravings under control. Before leaving the restaurant, I stop at the large grill where a chef is cooking another batch and thought that the next diners have no idea what will be in store for them.

A second day I tour the Islands of the Inland Sea, and again, I am startled by the gorgeous vistas while arriving by sea. The oyster beds are marked with pilings and they go on for miles off the shoreline. The hillsides abound in muted shades of green, and I understand why artists are inspired for their watercolors. The craggy coastline has a touch of Western New York here; although, these are mountainous areas and not rolling hills.

On Ikuchijima Island after lunch—a wooden decorative box with little draws opened up to small dishes of food—I tour the Ikuro Hirayama Museum of Art, with world famous works by the artist, who spent his boyhood on the island. A lot of his work is themed around the tragedy of the A-Bomb from his personal eyewitness experience—how could it not affect his life? —and his wish for promoting peace.

I am tranquil in a variety of settings—yes, even Hiroshima—and the parts of Japan's rural environs that visitors often miss staying in populated cities, will be several of the special areas I will remember.

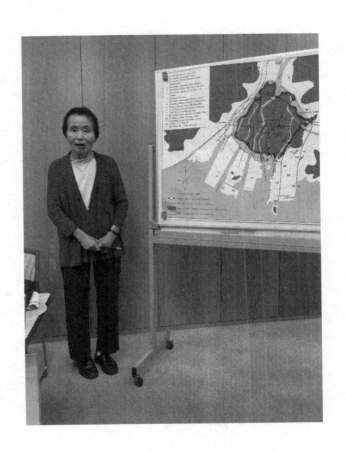

A Morning With Kids

It's a downright ordinary Sunday morning, except the forecast is predicting sunshine and unusually warm temperatures for mid May. In fact, the identical scene could be unfolding anywhere in the world. Parents, grandparents and young children decked out in oversized sunglasses, shorts, t-shirts and patterned sneakers are waiting in line, which becomes longer by the minute. The noise level is an octave above shrill with anticipation while the attention span of tons of munchkins is diminishing the longer the wait.

I mix into the line along with my travel mates, and we are completely out of place. We are not carrying a picnic basket, nor have a child or two in our arms. Actually, it is rather fun watching everybody from a distance without being personally involved. I'll get my kid fix this way.

A mom and dad with a set of boy twins around eighteen months—each holds one—has their hands full with two of everything required for an outing. One boy is a squirmy wiggle worm and when he is put down to toddle a bit, of course, he shoots off like a bull let out into the ring and flies away from his folks. His eyes are dancing when he looks back waiting for daddy to catch him. It's that age-old game. Dad races to scoop him up, and the scene happens over and over with first one and the other, gleeful in perfecting their escape arts. The parents are good-natured and do their upmost keeping the boys under control. I'm like the assorted older relatives in their group—aunties and grandparents—and leave the discipline to the parents. The older folks talk among themselves. It reminds me that once I was in the parents' shoes, too, and that's how I kept slim. Now there is no pressure to discipline kids.

Frankly, when I woke up in the morning, I wanted this to be a day for a little final introspection, and it doesn't look like it might happen. I'll take whatever is transpiring and go with it, though. There is no sense in being a scrooge. One thing I do appreciate about my choices in life is living in a multi generational community. It keeps me young and knowing what's the latest. When the neighbor kids or grandkids stop over, they make me smile with their energy and spirit. I love watching them grow up and seeing how they put their inquisitive minds to use in solving problems. Being in the country opens up doors to nature that town and city children don't have.

Our group outing is to Ikuchijima Island, part of the Inland Sea. My tour guide says, "Not to worry." The families will get off at the first stop on the ferry, Okunoshima Island, affectionately known as Rabbit Island, and we will have the boat to ourselves for the rest of the ride. That peeked my curiosity a bit and thought it is an amusement park. Well, it is in some ways until I picked up a travel brochure on the dock explaining where the children are going for frolicking.

Rabbit Island is home to hundreds of wild but friendly bunnies who are known to approach tourists in large groups to scavenge for food. And visitors are more than willing to get on the ground and allow the rabbits to crawl all over them—even though the damp patches on their clothes suggest the adorable animals have wet feet and potentially answered the call of nature while jumping all over their new friends. Okunoshima, is now a haven for friendly rabbits. It also provides a much needed counterbalance to the island's otherwise dark history—as the production site for Japan's chemical weapons during the Second World War.

Of course, Japan being the birthplace of kawaii, the distinct cultural appreciation of all things cute—the bounding herds of friendly rabbits are a much bigger attraction than the Poison Gas Museum. But although the source of the rabbits remains a mystery, it may be that the origin of the island's fluffy residents is intertwined with its history as manufacturer of chemical weapons. Between 1929-1945, the Japanese army secretly produced over 6,000 tons of poison gas on Okunoshima, which was removed from maps of the area and chosen because of its discreet location and distance from civilian populations. At the time, an unfortunate colony of rabbits was brought to the island in order to test the effects of the poison.

The ferryboat sips into the dock, we all get on in somewhat an orderly fashion, and pick seats for the best view. I find a spot near where the children have a recreational area and settle in watching the little ones jockeying for turns on the equipment. It is a lesson in child psychology observing how those children who are able to play well with others at a young age, will no doubt be better at working with others as grown ups. Take the tiny girl who grabs a plastic toy out of a bigger boy's hands and walks off while he stands there wondering what has happened. The parents intervene and smooth it out well I think. A school age girl sits by a couple people in my group, and they try talking with her. Her English is so limited they give up, she gets bored and moves back to next to her grandparents' bench. For what I am able to notice, kids are kids and no better or worse than at home. Young parents appear engaged and playful, too, and the emphasis appears to be on the kids. Dads are equally involved in child rearing, and the kids are alert to testing and trying whichever parent is the weaker link.

Sure enough, twenty minutes later and the multitudes are merrily off the boat and hopping down the bunny trails. As the first few families wind up the path, two or three bunnies come out to greet them. I hear squeals of laughter and I hope everyone has a wonderful Sunday together.

As the boat leaves the dock, and tranquility moves in where just a few minutes before there was a crush of people, I look out past the rolling water and let the sea breeze blow over my face. Refreshing.

Confusing Solitude With Loneliness

Just by the design of this trip and the choices that I make, I have little time for solitude; if you understand the term to mean seclusion, withdrawal and isolation from others.

That isn't the purpose of this trip to Japan to anyhow. I will be afforded other travel opportunities for soul-searching and being off on my own at a later date.

OAT offers active discovery vacations where learning takes place spontaneously. There is frequent contact with local people and a mix of socialization blended in to the program.

However, there are opportunities for me to withdraw into my own mind even though I am surrounded by people, like when I gaze out the window of the bullet train into nothingness except for where my imagination takes me, or wander through a garden behind everyone else repeating an exciting phrase over and over in my head.

It is often said that when you are with a writer you know well as a person, you can tell if he, or she is "writing" in his mind at that moment, and not one hundred percent into the conversation at hand. It can't be helped. It doesn't mean that the writer is rude and doesn't care to engage with you. If possible, he would rather be off sitting in his office on the computer composing a piece. That's the short and long of it. Probably writers are not high on the popularity charts.

I look forward to saying good night to my travel group early in the evening and heading to my room for a time to write on my blog and catch up on my email. There is a little organizing for the next day to stay a step of the game plan. And yes, there is hand laundry to do and drape artfully in the bathroom like an Irish washerwoman. I suppose you can say that is my daily solitude routine before I fall asleep. Since I am an early riser and each day is jammed packed, I need my rest.

Loneliness, which refers to a lack of companionship and is often associated with unhappiness, should not be confused with solitude, which is the state of being alone or cut off from all human contact. You can be in the midst of a crowd of people and still experience *loneliness*, but not *solitude*, since you are not physically alone.

When I first started traveling on my own regularly I would have a jab of loneliness right around the second Sunday, and I attribute it to missing my husband and nothing more. Somehow it never failed that in the very spot I was located, everyone nearby appeared to be part of a twosome, and here I had no one. Poor me. That sinking in my stomach would last for a short while and then fade away. I wouldn't let it cripple me, or take away the significant portion of the day. In Japan I mentally held on to thoughts to share later with my husband and didn't let myself get trapped into pity for being alone even for a second. I've matured.

Not So Easily Forgotten

I get as much satisfaction in reliving travel days and weeks later as I do the actual tours. When I return home, I appreciate having breathing room before going on to the next big activity, or short weekend trip. I refer to this interlude as a mandatory slowing down period for collecting my wits and cooling off from intense concentration. I am overwhelmed at how much I do remember, too. I can't imagine how my brain is able to store so much information. There are the little incidences, too, that make a lasting impression, and I am pulling up several right now.

A couple weeks after being home I am rereading my travel handbook that has a listing of tours day-by-day, and suddenly a clear picture of stopping in a convenience store one evening in Kyoto comes to mind. You won't believe this story. After searching the usual places in the aisles, I ask the salesperson where to find the gum, and he looks at me with the oddest facial expression and steps back away from the counter. Since I didn't get a response from the guy, I walked away a little perplexed. He misunderstands, and when I relate this to my tour guide, she clarifies that he saw an American and immediately thought that I wanted a gun. The proper way I am told is to ask for chewing gum. That totally scares me, and I don't refill my gum supply for the duration of my visit. Talk about a false notion about people that stereotypes everyone into one category.

My computer has issues getting on the network at the hotel in Tokyo after they routinely change their password at the beginning of a new month. My Mac Air wants to automatically connect to the older password. The front desk sends up a man who really doesn't understand what I need, and I have to make up an excuse after an hour that I must get to dinner so that he will give up. His brow is sweating from checking and rechecking the wiring behind the desk, which had nothing to do with the issue at hand. I repeat my problem over and over to him, and he is not catching on with his limited English.

It's his honor at stake. That evening, when he is at the front desk, he averts his eyes from mine embarrassed, and I let it go. I hope he doesn't remember me as pushy and rude.

I try again with two younger desk clerks, and have better luck. One copies off the Internet the Apple manual for my computer model on how to change a specific setting. She goes into the system preferences, it is done correctly and I thank her while she bows out of my room. I am good to go from then on until my iCloud storage announces that it is full. That's another problem, though, and I work on that one myself, keep calm and after returning home, I work with my tech person at MAC Ave to retrieve lost pictures.

There is no hair-raising episode about getting lost or a tale of forgetting which direction to turn for winding back the way I came. I must say that that's a first for me, too, and I attribute it to sheer luck. It's the exact opposite, and all twelve of we experienced travelers—not a clingy, dependent one in the lot—decide in unison that we are sticking like lemmings to our tour guide as she navigates the train and subway system in Tokyo no questions asked. It becomes quite obvious that not a one of us can decipher the rail system, and why waste the energy when we are with a guide who will pull us through the maze. Besides, she is used to being directive and we respond to her. So, picture Mother Duckling holding up her red flag, and a dozen little ducklings following all in a crooked row with nary a one stopping no matter what. Our eyes stay glued purposefully to the red flag, and when one or the other of us gets behind, someone is there to save our neck. The group effort is ideal. We head down the long set of stairs at the subway station, putting our ticket into the machine, taking it out and heading to the platform for our train. After leaving the train at our final stop, we insert our ticket and the machine eats it. We are so well trained and march like soldiers mouthing aloud the words, "Put your ticket in, and take your ticket out. Save your ticket and let the machine eat the ticket." Well, we were lightening up by the end of three weeks, and making the most of an impossibly difficult transportation task.

The morning after a temple tour in Kyoto—a crushing crowd of people closing in on me without a moment to stop and actually look—walking back to the bus, my eyes dart into a shop selling kimonos and I am in and out with an off-white one with dusty pink flowers wrapped up within five minutes.

I get a heads-up from my tour guide earlier on the trip, and I wait until Kyoto to find the best examples of kimonos in either polyester or silk depending upon how much I want to spend. Polyester and a cotton blend seem more practical to me. I happen to be in the right place at the right time, and any shopper knows the drill. Wait and you may regret it. I've been lounging in my new kimono at home and I feel very Eastern drinking loose green tea that I also brought back. The main reason for my visit to the temple is thwarted. I hurry away disappointed.

I am aware of a Japanese man in his forties at the military museum moving into our group and listening intently to our tour guide. He's dressed casually in a t-shirt and jeans, and a baseball cap. He follows along and when she pauses, he makes a comment in English. I can't quite hear what he says, and my tour guide doesn't give him any attention either. She has her plan, and like in most other situations, there is just so much time. This is the first time in the trip that we are bringing the war out in the open and hearing the Japanese perspective, and I am a little nervous. I assume that he is going to launch into some anti-American tirade, or a dig about our current political scene. It won't be the first time I've heard comments while in other countries. I brace myself and ignore him by moving to the back of our circle. I don't know what to expect. Apparently, he has nothing but good will. He begins by saying that he feels the same way about the war as our guide and all the younger generations In Japan. He wants us to know that. He breaks off from us, waves and I recognize that he is rational human being with a heart like mine.

I distinctly remember one early evening when I curl up on my bed in the hotel and use it to tell myself that I am in Japan. Feel it. Connect with it. I want to be by myself. I don't want any distractions, and I don't want to be distracted, because once there, my imagination is touched at its center, and the world becomes important and relevant. Ideas come out in a wallop and conversations in my head bounce all over like ping pong balls wacked back and forth over the net. Ideas need collecting. I take the abstract and make it concrete by playing with all my senses to get sharper descriptions. Sometimes I will grab my laptop and begin writing unaware of anything else within ten feet of me. Forgetting is not a concern, and I remain confident a phrase will resurface when it can be put to advantage in the future.

Most people have a special place or two if they are lucky where this occurs to a degree. It may be on a sunrise beach walk, miles into a hiking trail, or in a worship service. Lots of times it is in a brand new place that touches you and brings a flood of emotions to the surface.

I am having so many of these high moments here in Japan that my brain is flooded and agitated. I find no escape route and only pray that my daily adventures can find vacant space to be sucked inside my brain. I am practiced in the art of seeing more than the average person, and like a photographer whose best shots are off at an angle, I tilt the world in my writing in a very personal way, and more importantly, create universal truth. What a person sees from a distance, a writer sees through a microscope. Writers train themselves to seek this moment more often than other people, and that is why a writer goes from periods of doing the usual social stuff with friends and family to days and weeks of isolation. The kitchen counter goes an additional day piled higher and the weeds in the garden are not removing themselves without assistance. It is a writer's method of coping.

"The impulse to create begins—often terribly and fearfully—in a tunnel of silence." – Adrienne Rich.

Cranes Everywhere

What on earth does that phrase mean? Cranes, the oldest birds in the world, are omens for everything, and anything.

Crane mythology is wide spread and can be found in many cultures, including Japan. The crane is one of the mystical or holy creatures (others include the dragon and the tortoise) and symbolizes good fortune and longevity because of its fabled life span of a thousand years.

At the Narukawa Art Museum in Hakone, cranes are the theme in several watercolors, woodcuts and folding screens in the collection. Between studying their stately presence and sitting in the lounge looking out the massive picture window at Mount Fuji in full view, I am pleased to be where I am at this point in my life. Nothing is perfect, nor will it ever be on earth. I *am* satisfied with the choices that I have made. And it possibly could be right here that the first notion that I am saturating my senses with my travels to Japan occurs, and I will need to get them down on paper.

The crane is a favorite subject in the tradition of origami or paper folding. An ancient Japanese legend promises that anyone who folds a thousand paper cranes will be granted a wish by a crane (see the chapter on Hiroshima and Beyond).

Truly global citizens, the world's fifteen species of cranes range freely over five continents and migrate across deserts, mountains, frozen tundra, and the borders of hundreds of nations. As such, they are ambassadors for peace among diverse peoples, who unite in efforts to save the elegant birds, and for the preservation of their fragile wetland and grassland homes and migratory staging grounds. Because of development and habitat loss, many species that once thrived in much broader ranges, including the Red-crowned, Black-crowned, and White-naped Cranes, are now restricted to fragments of protected land in parks, sanctuaries, and even demilitarized zones between hostile nations.

By definition, peace is an occurrence of harmony characterized by the lack of violence, conflict behaviors and the freedom of fear of violence. Peace also suggests sincere attempts at reconciliation, the existence of interpersonal or international relationships, and a working political order that serves the true interests of all.

Living with an imperfect past and moving into a new century, collectively the Japanese people, in my way of thinking, are keeping peace at the forefront. Like the crane, it could become endangered unless the practice of understanding of what it means to strive for peace is not kept at the forefront of history discussions in the classroom. Through youth we have our future. Although the economy has tanked these past twenty years, and it is not as prosperous as it once was in the 80s, that has not gotten in the way of efforts to maintain a stability within the country.

There is a major pressure on individuals to be successful. Once I sat across from a suited young man on a train, and my friend nudged my arm to take a closer look at him while he was glued to his cell phone. He had a nervous twitch and a shake of his shoulder that would show periodically. That's stress. Another time I was on a different train with a group of teens coming back from a soccer match. They were standing for over a half hour at the front of the train. A couple of the boys slept standing, no doubt from exhaustion. There is never enough time to rest and kick back for a Japanese student. That's stress, too.

There are many versions of the Japanese folktale about a woman who is in fact a crane disguised as a human. To make money the crane-woman plucks her own feathers to weave silk brocade. It provides money when sold, but the crane-woman becomes increasingly ill as she does. When her true identity is discovered and the nature of her illness, she flies away. Look up into the sky today and you imagine her floating overhead. Cranes are everywhere.

I am like a crane in my travels, sticking my neck out taking in all that I am able for hours and hours through all kinds of conditions. I put in a regular five to seven miles of walking a day and climb stairs sometimes fifty at a time in diverse climates and weather conditions.

My all-time absolute, soul-rendering trip was to Ireland. I can't deny it was the shock of a lifetime to be so invested into the culture. Ah, the sweet music and stories which rolled off the tongues of solid Irishmen wherever I stepped into a pub like I was a friend for life newly arrived from America and no questions asked. It is good fortune that Ireland was my first solo traveling experience of recent years. The country delights in visitors and is reasonably safe. I am thinking positive thoughts and sending up wishes to fly with the cranes for a return visit. I want to write my heart away while absorbing the landscape and pub scene somewhere on the Western shore.

The second greatest trip was with my husband to view the antiquities in Egypt. The timing was just right a couple months before the people's uprising. Again, the stars were aligned just right, and we had the blessings of the cranes.

And now, Japan ranks number three. That bowing gets me every time. Seriously, the order and awareness that the Japanese people approach their temporary journeys on earth is remarkable. It is my introduction to an Asian country, and I choose a treasure.

Why do I travel? For escape. For rejuvenation. For fresh starts. For imagined high romance. For mystery. All of the above mentioned. I have been itching to go somewhere all my life. At eight or nine, I couldn't wait to go on the train with my dad when he did business in New York City. I dove into maps and wanted to understand how to get around the city like a grow up. Coming back from my first all-day trip to the city, I hardly could sleep at night from the larger world I had discovered beyond my bedroom window. The quest never stops, and my childlike daydream continues into adulthood.

A friend wonders if I am ever afraid to travel on my own. I have a sneaking suspicion that others think the same thought without saying it to my face. That's a personality trait of mine, and also, I capitalize on it, taking all the appropriate precautions into account.

Don't get be wrong. I do like being at home, too, and locally sourced home-cooked meals. I am a reader, writer and avid walker. Theatre and musical evenings are a big part of my entertaining schedule, along with dining at places in the region. It is important for me to maintain ties in my community and participate in organizations for the betterment of all citizens. Friendships have a role, too, in rounding me out, and I love a night of stimulating conversation around a table.

The truth of the matter is that I am at ease knowing I have one or two trips in the planning stages down the road. I am like a crane in that I am ready to take flight and spread my wings at the drop of a hat.

I figure situations out, take the first step and watch how things unfold. Each trip I go on I don't know anybody—it's exciting to me—and return with many new friends who I keep in touch with thanks to email and Facebook. On a trip to Spain in 2015 I did meet a friend who traveled with me to Japan, and we will continue on with more trips in the future together. We click, and both of us leave the other room to be independent, too.

Since writing my first travel book four years ago, *A Smidgen of Irish Luck,* I have developed an approach to solo travel within a group framework that works satisfactorily. On the other hand, I am fine traveling with my husband, too, depending on the situation. He and I have common interests including an almost impossible mission of uncovering every rock and seeing the maximum when we tour. We return home exhausted and happy.

This particular trip requires more preparation and study, compact packing and an open mind to handling differences on an adventure. I believe I passed with flying colors thanks to the good omen of a crane.

Japan is a transformative experience. If nothing else, the cranes are teaching me to settle into more quietness one day at a time and continue reaching out beyond my tent poles, for there is a huge expanse of earth waiting for me.

ACKNOWLEDGMENTS

Thank you, Japanese people, for making me feel most welcome in your exquisite country. I cannot say enough.

Thanks to Overseas Adventure Travel for putting all the details in place adding up for a smooth trip with my tour director, Mariko Enoki.

This labor of love could not have happened, and within such a tight deadline, too, without the experienced editing skills of Kate Stiffler. I appreciate the teamwork, Kate.

Larry, your belief in my ability is so absolute, despite flimsy evidence. Your comments after a first reading gave me the strength to reach higher.

Thanks to Beth Doty Designs, Geneseo, NY for my professional portrait. Beth, you make my eyes sparkle and my smile come alive.

If you would like to see pictures in color from the entire trip with a little commentary, go to my blog, Tour Japan With Kay http://tourjapanwithkay.blogsport.com

Made in the USA
Middletown, DE
12 October 2016